Lucifer

The Divine Comedy

Lucifer

The Divine Comedy

Mike Carey
Writer

Peter Gross
Ryan Kelly
Dean Ormston
Artists

Daniel Vozzo
Colorist

Comicraft
Letterer

Christopher Moeller
Original Series Covers

Based on characters created by
Neil Gaiman, Sam Kieth and
Mike Dringenberg

LUCIFER: THE DIVINE COMEDY

DC Comics, 1700 Broadway, New York, NY 10019

A division of Warner Bros. - An AOL Time Warner Company

Printed in Canada. First Printing.

ISBN: 1-4012-0009-5

Cover illustrations by Christopher Moeller

THE SILVER CITY HAS NEITHER GUARDS NOR BATTLEMENTS.
IT DOES NOT NEED THEM. THE PERVERSE AND TERRIBLE BRIGHTNESS OF ITS BUILDINGS WOULD BLIND ANY INTRUDER.
AND THE ROOM CALLED THE LOGOS, IN THE TOWER UNENDINGLY HIGH--THAT, TOO, IS UNGUARDED.
THERE ARE NOT MANY WHO WOULD WILLINGLY SEEK IT OUT.
YOU WOULD SAY IT IS AN EMPTY ROOM. BUT YOU WOULD BE WRONG.
WHEN GOD CHOOSES TO SPEAK, THIS IS WHERE HIS VOICE SOUNDS.
SO IT IS FULL OF WORDS. FOR GOD'S VOICE DOES NOT DECAY.
THE MILLION-THROATED SUSURRUS OF THOSE WORDS INDUCES CONFUSION AND MADNESS.
FATHER, HEAR ME! I AM TROUBLED AND I COME TO YOU FOR GUIDANCE.
BUT THE ARCHANGEL MICHAEL IS PROOF AGAINST THEM.
MY BROTHER LUCIFER HAS DEFIED YOUR EDICT AND SEEKS A RECKONING WITH YOU.
HOW CAN I AVOID FURTHER CONFLICT?

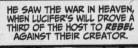

AND GOD *SPAKE* UNTO MICHAEL, IN THE TONGUE THAT ANGELS SPEAK.

AND MICHAEL SAW WHAT HAD BEEN, AND WHAT WAS, AND WHAT WOULD BE.

HE SAW THE WAR IN HEAVEN, WHEN LUCIFER'S WILL DROVE A THIRD OF THE HOST TO *REBEL* AGAINST THEIR CREATOR.
THE WAR IN WHICH HE HIMSELF HAD BEEN WOUNDED AND TAKEN PRISONER.

HE SAW LUCIFER RULING HELL-- AND *CHAFING* BECAUSE WHILE HE RULED HE WAS A *SUBJECT,* TOO.
BECAUSE ALL HIS POWER BROUGHT HIM NOT ONE *STEP* CLOSER TO HIS TRUE GOAL.

THAT IS WHY HE *LEFT,* OF COURSE. WHY HE GAVE AWAY THE KEY TO HELL AND RETIRED TO EARTH.
BECAUSE HE KNEW THAT HE WAS NOT FREE, AND IT HURT HIS DIGNITY TO *DANCE* ON THE END OF A LEASH.

BUT THEN HEAVEN CALLED HIM BACK INTO ITS EMPLOY, USING THE ONLY BRIBE THAT WOULD EVER HAVE *WORKED* ON HIM.
A LETTER OF PASSAGE. A POTENTIAL *EXIT* FROM GOD'S CREATION.

HE SLEW THE VOICELESS GODS, AND WON HIS PRIZE-- THEN USED IT, NOT TO *LEAVE,* BUT TO OPEN A GATEWAY INTO THE VOID.
AND GOD WATCHED, SERENELY, FROM THE VANTAGE POINT OF ETERNITY. THIS, TOO WAS *FORESEEN.*

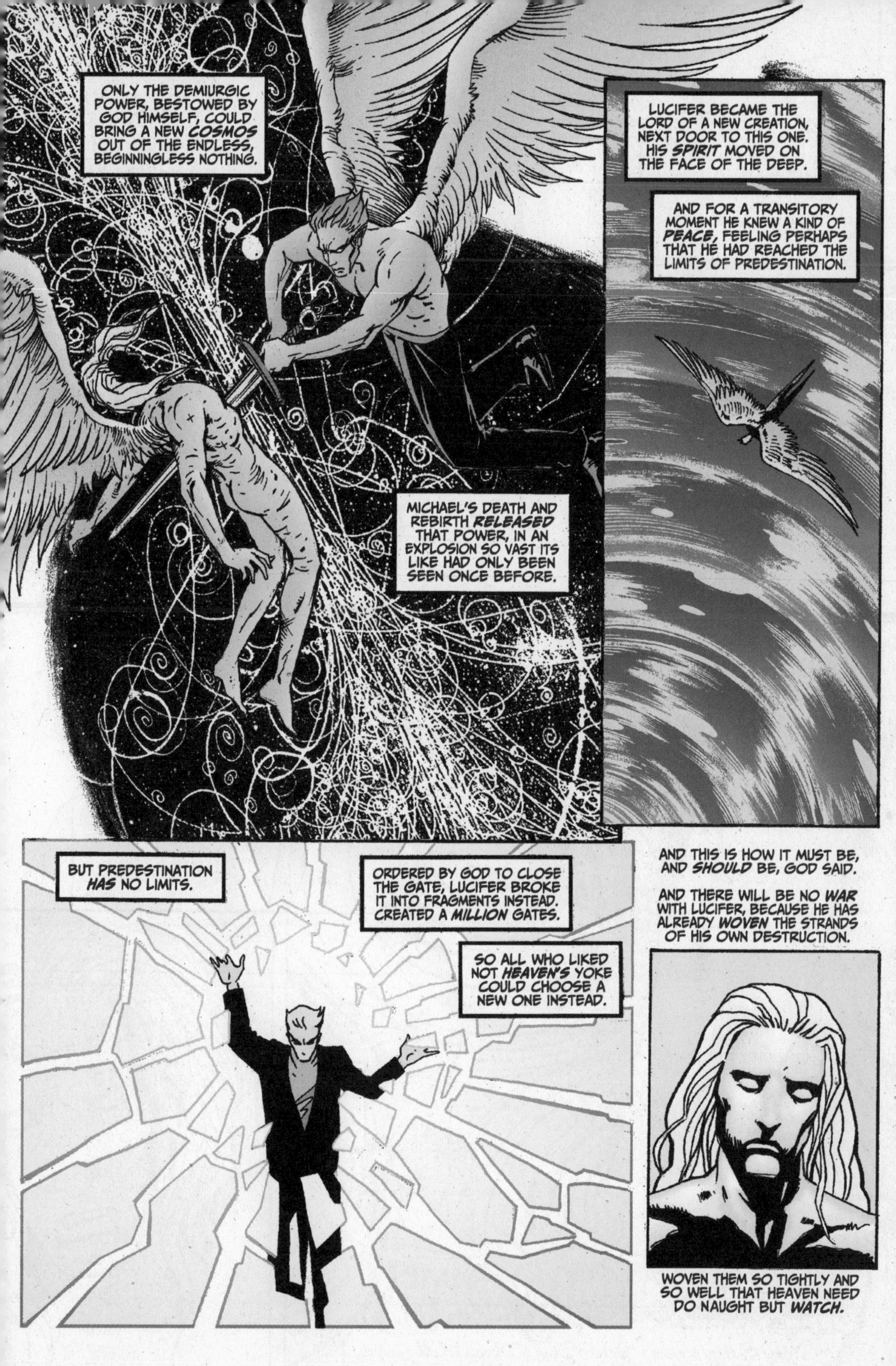
ONLY THE DEMIURGIC POWER, BESTOWED BY GOD HIMSELF, COULD BRING A NEW COSMOS OUT OF THE ENDLESS, BEGINNINGLESS NOTHING.
MICHAEL'S DEATH AND REBIRTH RELEASED THAT POWER, IN AN EXPLOSION SO VAST ITS LIKE HAD ONLY BEEN SEEN ONCE BEFORE.
LUCIFER BECAME THE LORD OF A NEW CREATION, NEXT DOOR TO THIS ONE. HIS SPIRIT MOVED ON THE FACE OF THE DEEP.
AND FOR A TRANSITORY MOMENT HE KNEW A KIND OF PEACE, FEELING PERHAPS THAT HE HAD REACHED THE LIMITS OF PREDESTINATION.
BUT PREDESTINATION HAS NO LIMITS.
ORDERED BY GOD TO CLOSE THE GATE, LUCIFER BROKE IT INTO FRAGMENTS INSTEAD. CREATED A MILLION GATES.
SO ALL WHO LIKED NOT HEAVEN'S YOKE COULD CHOOSE A NEW ONE INSTEAD.
AND THIS IS HOW IT MUST BE, AND SHOULD BE, GOD SAID.
AND THERE WILL BE NO WAR WITH LUCIFER, BECAUSE HE HAS ALREADY WOVEN THE STRANDS OF HIS OWN DESTRUCTION.
WOVEN THEM SO TIGHTLY AND SO WELL THAT HEAVEN NEED DO NAUGHT BUT WATCH.

MUST IT BE SO, LORD?
MY BROTHER HAS CHOSEN HIS PATH, BUT MUST INNOCENTS SUFFER TOO?
AND YES, GOD SAID. IT MUST BE SO, AND IT SHALL BE SO.
TO WISH OTHERWISE WERE BLASPHEMY.
THE ARCHANGEL STARED DOWN INTO THE IMMENSITY OF CREATION, WHICH SEEMED BLURRED AND SPANGLED, SEEN THROUGH AN UNFAMILIAR VEIL.
AND IN SOME CORNER OF HIS VAST AND FAITHFUL HEART--
--A BLASPHEMY WAS BORN.
Paradiso part 1 of 3
Mike Carey writer • Peter Gross & Ryan Kelly artists
Daniel Vozzo colorist & separations • Comicraft lettering
Christopher Moeller cover painting
Mariah Huehner assistant editor • Shelly Bond editor
Based on characters created by Gaiman, Kieth & Dringenberg

THE FIORENZE, LAS VEGAS.

I WANT THE FAME, THE MONEY AND YOU. NOTHING LESS WILL DO. NOTHING LESS WILL DOOOO.

JILL PRESTO, LIVE ON STAGE.

CLAPCLAPCLAP
PHWEET PHWEET

THANK YOU.

THANK YOU ALL.

YEAH!

YOU'VE BEEN GREAT, GUYS. I MEAN IT. I'LL BE BACK IN A COUPLE OF HOURS WITH SOME SONGS FROM THE NEW ALBUM.
MEANWHILE, IF YOU'RE GOING TO THE TABLES WHISPER MY NAME FOR LUCK, YOU HEAR?

THANKS, AVROM. ANYTHING NEW?

A GUY OFFERED ME A C-NOTE FOR YOUR G-STRING. EDDIE SAYS HE'S BOOKED A TABLE AT SWALE'S. AND YOUR MOM CALLED AGAIN.

IF YOU DON'T CHANGE THE NAME OF THE ALBUM SHE SAYS SHE'S GOING TO SUE YOUR ASS.

LET HER TRY. I'VE GOT THE RIGHTS TO THOSE SONGS. EVERYTHING SHE EVER DID.

AND EVERY TIME SHE TURNS ON THE RADIO SHE'S GONNA HEAR ME SINGING THEM.

YEAH, I LOVE THAT FAMILY THING YOU GOT GOING THERE. IT CHOKES ME UP.

...HAS SELDOM SEEN SUCH A METEORIC RISE: FROM THE MARGINAL TO THE MAGNIFICENT IN ONE SHORT YEAR.
PRESTO'S DEBUT ALBUM, "OPEN SESAME," CAME OUT OF LEFT FIELD LAST SUMMER TO SOAR TO THE TOP OF THE ALBUM CHARTS IN A SCANT THREE WEEKS.
NOW HER LATEST OFFERING, "STARS DON'T SHINE," IS SET TO WIN THIS CABARET-CIRCUIT VETERAN HER FIRST PLATINUM DISK.

SO IS JILL PRESTO "REFRESHINGLY FRANK AND OPEN" OR "SO BRASH SHE MAKES EVEN NEW YORKERS WINCE"?

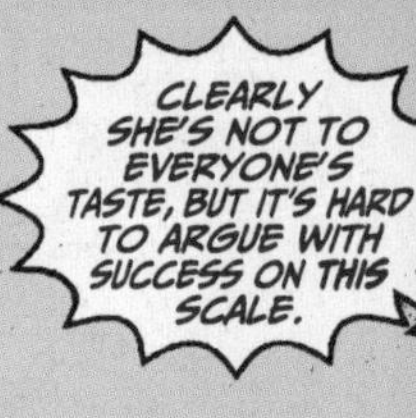
CLEARLY SHE'S NOT TO EVERYONE'S TASTE, BUT IT'S HARD TO ARGUE WITH SUCCESS ON THIS SCALE.

THE LADY'S GOT ENERGY AND AMBITION TO BURN, AND HER VEGAS STAGE SHOW IS PLAYING TO PACKED--
YOU KNOW, MAYBE I'LL FRAME THIS MAGAZINE COVER AND SEND IT TO HER ON MOTHER'S DAY.
WHAT DO YOU THINK?
Showtime

WE THINK IT HAS A FLAVOR OF PETTY SADISM.

BUT THEN IT'S HARDLY OUR PLACE TO JUDGE.

WELL MET IN VEGAS, JILL PRESTO.
ONCE AGAIN THE BASANOS MUST ACT WITH YOU, AND THROUGH YOU.
WELL, LOOK. IT... IT'S NOT EASY FOR ME TO GET AWAY RIGHT NOW.
I'M BOOKED THROUGH SUMMER. I'VE GOT COMMITMENTS HERE.
YOU HAVE WHAT WE HAVE GIVEN YOU.
AND WE WERE ALWAYS VERY CLEAR ABOUT THE PRICE.
EEARRRGHH!
PRESTO
THE HOUR OF OUR GLORY IS AT HAND, JILL.
BUT FIRST COMES THE STRUGGLE.
FOR US TO RISE, THE MORNINGSTAR MUST FALL. AGAIN.

"...AND THE FUTURE WILL PIVOT ON THE SMALLEST AND MOST INSIGNIFICANT OF HINGES."
BISHOP LAUD
I DON'T KNOW. IF I STAND AT AN ANGLE AND LEAN FORWARD YOU CAN SORT OF SEE THEM.
NO, YOU CAN SEE THEM. THEY'RE DEFINITELY BIGGER.
LISTEN, SARA. IS IT OKAY IF WE REVISE ROUND YOURS TONIGHT?
IT'S JUST TOO WEIRD AT MY HOUSE. MUM'S AT WORK ALL THE TIME AND DAD NEVER TALKS TO ME ANYMORE.
OKAY. BUT DEAD ON SEVEN, YEAH? WE'LL WORK FOR AN HOUR, THEN PLAY BOGGLE.
YEAH. OKAY.
SHE WAS AN EXPERIMENT, ELAINE BELLOC. AN ILL-CONCEIVED ATTEMPT TO CROSS TWO BLOODLINES BEST KEPT APART.
ON HER MOTHER'S SIDE, HUMAN AND STAINED. ON HER FATHER'S--
IMMACULATE. AN ANGEL.
GRACE AND PERFECTION AND ETERNITY WERE HER HERITAGE.
ALONG WITH THE WILL TO FLY BEYOND HER STRENGTH.
AND A SOUL SO BRIGHT IT COULD BE SEEN FROM HELL.

WHAT A TOTAL FRIGGING WASTE OF *TIME*.
WH... WHAT? WHAT DO YOU MEAN? WHY ARE YOU *WATCHING* ME?
NOT BECAUSE IT'S *FUN*, BELIEVE ME. YOU FLY LIKE SOMETHING FLAILING ON A *GIBBET*.
SPEAKING OF GIBBETS, BY THE WAY, YOU'RE ABOUT AN *HOUR* AWAY FROM AN AGONIZING DEATH.
BUT, HEY, DON'T LET *THAT* GET IN THE WAY OF THE BATSHIT AEROBATICS.
IT'S ALL THE SAME TO ME. YOU *CROAK*, I'M OFF THE HOOK IN ANY CASE.
BUT IF YOU DO WANT TO *LIVE* TO SEE YOUR THIRTEENTH BIRTHDAY, FOLLOW MY FRIGGING LIGHTS.
FIGURE OF *SPEECH*, YOU UNDERSTAND.

IT HAD BEGUN.
ACROSS THE CITIES AND THE DESERTS OF EARTH, ACROSS THE REALMS OF LIGHT AND THE REALMS OF PAIN, THE GATES WERE SCATTERED.
WELDED OPEN BY GOD'S OWN NAME.

ALL WHO SOUGHT THEM FOUND THEM NOW, AS IRON FILINGS FIND A LODESTONE.
AS WITH THE SILVER CITY, THIS WAS A LAND WHOSE FRONTIERS WERE UNDEFENDED.

IN ONES, IN TWOS, AFRAID AND UNAFRAID, WITH OR WITHOUT BACKWARD GLANCES, THEY PASSED THROUGH--
--AND WERE GONE.

LUCIFER WATCHED THEIR PROGRESS WITH DETACHED INTEREST.
HE CARED NOTHING FOR THEM AS INDIVIDUALS.
BUT IN THEIR STEADY ACCUMULATION HE SAW THE GRADUAL SHIFTING OF A COSMIC CONSTANT.

IT CAME DOWN TO THIS AT LAST. AFTER THE ENDLESS SCRABBLING FOR PURCHASE AND PURPOSE.
THINGS WERE EITHER BLACK OR WHITE. HE WOULD BE HIMSELF.
OR HE WOUL
BE NOTHING

EURGHH! AFTER THIS, WE'RE SQUARE, RIGHT?
YOU WON'T BE WANTING ANY MORE LITTLE FAVORS?
PUT THE HEART IN THE CENTER. ARRANGE THE OTHER VISCERA AT THE FOUR CARDINAL POINTS.
MAKE SURE NOTHING SPILLS OVER THE EDGE OF THE CIRCLE.
I MEAN, THIS IS THE AMBASSADOR SUITE. TOM JONES SLEPT--
ANOINT YOUR FACE WITH BLOOD. AND SPEAK THE WORDS WE TAUGHT YOU.
CONVOCO QUOD CARNIS NON TEGIT. IN SIGNUM RELIGO QUOD SIGNA NON LEGIT.
SINE FORMA, SINE VITA, SINE VOCE, SINE SPE...
SI VIS VULTUM, VENI AD ME!
OH, AND DAVE WHOSIS FROM EURHYTHMICS. HE SLEPT HERE, TOO.
RIGHT.
YOU WANT ME TO CALL ROOM SERVICE?

WHY...
HAVE YOU...
BROUGHT ME...BACK?
HWKCHH!
YOU ARE TOHU VEVOHU--WITHOUT FORM AND VOID.
BUT WE CAN GIVE YOU BACK ALL YOU'VE LOST, IF YOU WILL BE OUR AGENT IN A CERTAIN MATTER.

WHAT MATTER?
A MATTER IN WHICH, FOR THE TIME BEING, OUR HAND MUST BE CONCEALED.
IT CONCERNS LUCIFER, IF YOU STILL REMEMBER THAT NAME.
I REMEMBER NOTHING.
I WANT TO KNOW MYSELF. I WANT MY FACE BACK.
IT SEEMS I SHOULD NOT TRUST YOU. BUT I WILL AGREE TO YOUR TERMS.
THEN IT SHALL BE SO.
GO FROM THIS PLACE AS YOURSELF. AND DO OUR BIDDING.
I... I'M GONNA LEAVE NOW, OKAY?
I'VE GOT ANOTHER SET TO DO.
A PERFORMANCE? NO. THAT'S NOT POSSIBLE.
YOU NEED TO RENT A CAR. YOU HAVE A JOURNEY TO GO ON.
BUT I DON'T EVEN DRIVE!
THEN ARRANGE SOME OTHER TRANSPORT. WE'LL NEED YOU FOR A FEW HOURS MORE.
OR FOR A THOUSAND YEARS.
IT DEPENDS HOW YOU COUNT.

YOU'VE BEEN LOOKING FOR A NEW WORLD, AND NOW YOU'VE FOUND IT. CONGRATULATIONS.
AND A WORD OF WARNING.
REMEMBER THAT MY HAND IS OUTSTRETCHED ABOVE YOU--IN A LITERAL, NOT A METAPHORICAL SENSE.
THERE ARE CERTAIN THINGS I WON'T TOLERATE.
DON'T BRING THE HABIT OF WORSHIP HERE WITH YOU.
GRAVEN IMAGES, ANTHROPOMORPHIZED ABSTRACTIONS, COSMIC PRINCIPLES; THEY'RE ALL EQUALLY UNACCEPTABLE.
THOSE OF YOU WHO ARE HIDING BEHIND HUMAN SEEMINGS, YOU CAN KEEP THEM-- BUT REMEMBER THAT I SEE THROUGH YOUR FACES. I KNOW EXACTLY WHAT YOU ARE.
IF YOU SET UP CHURCHES OR CALL YOURSELVES GODS I'LL DESTROY YOU.
THAT'S ALL. I DON'T BELIEVE IN DOVES OR COVENANTS. YOU'LL KNOW YOU'VE DISPLEASED ME--
--IF THE SKY TURNS BLACK.

I HAD A VISION, MAN. I SAW A FUCKING ANGEL STANDING IN THE SUN!
WE ALL DID.
AND WE ALL HEARD WHAT HE SAID.
THE HABIT OF WORSHIP...
I GUESS THAT'S IT, THEN. WE'RE FREE.
I WONDER WHICH ANGEL HE IS.
GIVEN HIS VIEWS ON RELIGION--
--I'D SAY THAT'S PRETTY OBVIOUS.

HEY! HEY YOU, KID! DIDN'T YOU HEAR ME?
I'VE BEEN SENT TO LEAD YOU TO SAFETY.
LONSDALE STREET
SENT BY WHO?
UHH... BY LUCIFER, OF COURSE.
I MEAN, CHECK OUT THE WINGS. YOU CAN SEE I'M NOT LOCAL TALENT, RIGHT? YOU CAN TRUST ME.
I SAW CREATURES LIKE YOU WHEN I WAS IN HELL.
WHOA! LOOK-DON'T-TOUCH! LOOK- DON'T-TOUCH!
AND I KNOW LUCIFER DOESN'T LIVE IN HELL ANYMORE.
SO I DON'T TRUST YOU. AT ALL.
I THINK YOU WANT TO LEAD ME OFF INTO THE DARK TO SOME PLACE WHERE YOUR FRIENDS ARE WAITING.
GGGGLCK!
AND I'M NOT FALLING FOR IT!
ALL RIGHT, YOU SNOT-NOSED LITTLE BITCH! I WARNED YOU!
YOU EVER SEEN ROADKILL? BECAUSE THAT'S WHAT YOU'RE GONNA LOOK LIKE! THEY'RE GONNA HAVE TO IDENTIFY YOU BY YOUR KIRLIAN AURA!
SHIT.

ARE YOU GOING TO TELL ME WHERE WE'RE *GOING* NOW?
UP THAT WAY. IT'S GOOD OF YOU TO DRIVE ME, ALBIE.
EDDIE.
EDDIE.
I HAD US A TABLE AT *SWALE'S* 'N' EVERYTHING, YOU KNOW?
I *KNOW* YOU DID, HONEY. I *SWEAR* I'LL MAKE IT UP TO YOU.
TELL HIM TO STOP WHERE THE ROAD TURNS.
AT THE CORNER THERE, *SWEETHEART.* EDDIE. OKAY?
DON'T SEE WHY YOU NEED TO COME OUT TO THE DESERT JUST 'CAUSE YOU'RE WRITING A *SONG* ABOUT IT, JILL.
I MEAN, IT'S JUST A DESERT. Y'ALREADY *KNOW* WHAT IT LOOKS LIKE.
THAT'S THE THING WE SAW IN L.A. THE GATEWAY. HOW DID IT GET WAY OUT *HERE?*
WHAT?
TELL HIM HE IS TO REMAIN IN THE CAR.
THE GATEWAY IS WHERE IT *ALWAYS* IS. THIS IS ONLY A *FRAGMENT* OF IT, FOLDED THROUGH SPACE.
FOR THE LAST HUNDRED FEET THE TRAIL IS QUITE NARROW. TAKE IT *SLOWLY.*

LET ME *HUFF* GET THIS STRAIGHT. YOU WANT ME TO GO *IN* THERE?
IN A LITTLE WHILE, YES.
AND DO *WHAT*, EXACTLY?
IT WOULD DO YOU NO GOOD TO KNOW.
WELL, I WANT TO KNOW ANYWAY. I'M NOT FLYING *BLIND* ANY-MORE.
GIVE ME THE BIG *PICTURE* OR I'M GOING BACK TO VEGAS.
THE BIG PICTURE WOULD FALL ON YOUR MIND LIKE A *MOUNTAIN*.
LET ME SHOW YOU.
BARROOOOM
PERHAPS YOU *WILL* GO BACK.
BUT IT WILL NOT BE BY *THIS* ROAD.

YOU'RE LATE. WHAT HAPPENED?
I HAD TO SORT OUT SOME OLD RUBBISH. SORRY.
HI, ELAINE.
THE TYPE OF ENERGY POSSESSED BY A BODY THAT'S RAISED ABOVE ITS ORIGINAL HEIGHT IS--
KINETIC ENERGY.
POTENTIAL ENERGY.
OH, YEAH. POTENTIAL ENERGY.

THE TYPE OF ENERGY POSSESSED BY A BODY IN--
NOK NOK
OH, WHAT'S THE POINT OF SAYING SEVEN O'CLOCK IF EVERYONE COMES WHEN THEY LIKE?

SO...UMM...YOU KNOW THEY'RE SHOWING THE ORIGINAL STAR WARS TRILOGY AT THE PHOENIX?
OH YEAH? THEY DID THAT LAST YEAR TOO.
IF YOU LIKE, WE COULD GO SEE IT.

ELAINE! IT'S YOUR DAD. HE SAID--
OW!

GET YOUR COAT.
YOU'RE COMING HOME.

DAD! I'M JUST DOING SOME HOMEWORK. I'LL BE BACK BEFORE TEN. IT'S OKAY.
NO. NO, IT ISN'T OKAY. DO YOU THINK I'M AN IDIOT?
DO YOU THINK I DON'T KNOW WHAT YOU DID?
YOU MADE A PACT WITH LUCIFER. YOU KISSED HIS RING, YOU SIGNED YOUR NAME IN HIS BOOK.

NO! I DIDN'T DO ANYTHING LIKE THAT! I DON'T KNOW WHAT YOU MEAN!
OF COURSE YOU DON'T. LITTLE MISS INNOCENT.
THE DEVIL'S WHORE.

MR. BELLOC, THAT'S NOT RIGHT. YOU SHOULDN'T--
SPEAK ONE MORE WORD TO ME, BOY, AND I'LL RIP YOUR FUCKING TONGUE OUT.

THE DEVIL'S WHORE. THE DEVIL'S BITCH.
DON'T SAY THAT! IT'S NOT TRUE.
HE'S JUST MY FRIEND!

YOUR FRIEND? THEN MAYBE YOU SHOULD RUN OFF AND PLAY WITH YOUR FRIEND--
--AND LET THE REST OF US GLUE OUR FUCKING LIVES BACK TOGETHER!

IF I COULD, I WOULD, RIGHT NOW!
BUT HE'S IN ANOTHER UNIVERSE, MAKING WORLDS.
WELL THAT'S GOOD.
THAT'S VERY GOOD.
IS HE?
WE'RE NOT LIKELY TO BE INTERRUPTED THEN, ARE WE?
To Be Continued...

IN THE HOUSE OF WINDOWLESS ROOMS IN THE ROOM OF TRAVELING INWARD, WHOSE WALLS ARE MADE FROM HIS FATHER'S SKIN, SUSANO-O-NO-MIKOTO HAD SAT FOR ONE HUNDRED DAYS.
THIS WAS TO BE THE LAST DAY, BUT HE DID NOT KNOW IT YET. HE WAS FORBIDDEN TO COUNT.

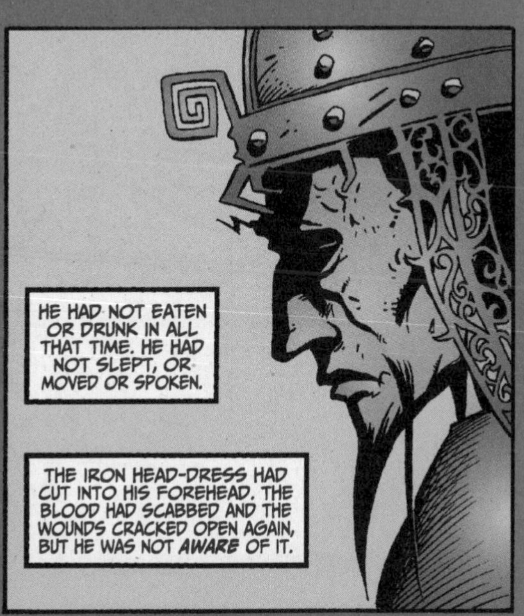
HE HAD NOT EATEN OR DRUNK IN ALL THAT TIME. HE HAD NOT SLEPT, OR MOVED OR SPOKEN.
THE IRON HEAD-DRESS HAD CUT INTO HIS FOREHEAD. THE BLOOD HAD SCABBED AND THE WOUNDS CRACKED OPEN AGAIN, BUT HE WAS NOT AWARE OF IT.

SERVANTS CREPT IN SILENTLY EVERY SECOND DAY.
THEY FED THE BIRDS, AND CLEANED AWAY THEIR DROPPING.

THEY TENDED THE BRAZIER, TOO. BURNED WORMWOOD AND ACONITE TO MAKE SUSANO'S DREAMS MORE BITTER AND MORE POTENT.
COALS FROM HINAZU TO KEEP THE BLADES RED-HOT.

HIS MIND WAS FOCUSED ON LUCIFER, HIS ENEMY-- FOR WHOM, PARADOXICALLY, HE NOW FELT A CERTAIN LOVE, BECAUSE HE KNEW HIM SO WELL.
BUT THAT WAS AN ACCIDENT OF THE DEATH-TRANCE. IT WOULD VANISH WHEN HE WOKE, AND HE WOULD NOT REMEMBER IT.

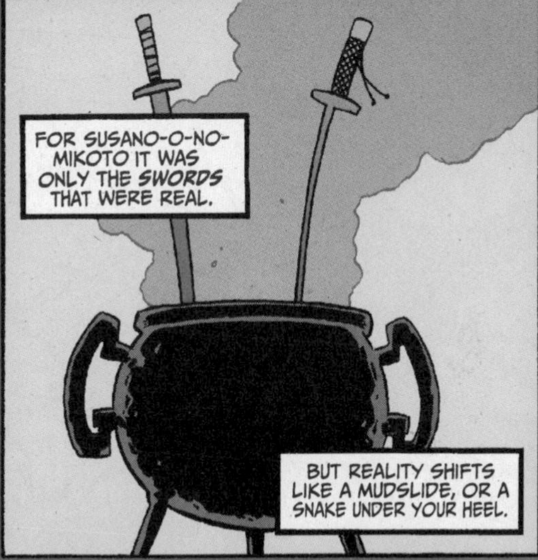
FOR SUSANO-O-NO-MIKOTO IT WAS ONLY THE SWORDS THAT WERE REAL.
BUT REALITY SHIFTS LIKE A MUDSLIDE, OR A SNAKE UNDER YOUR HEEL.

EVEN WHEN, LIKE ELAINE BELLOC, YOU THINK YOUR FOOTING IS FIRM.
YOU HAVE SUCH PRETTY HAIR.
AND YOU'RE SO SMALL. LIKE A DOLL.
IT'S HARD TO BELIEVE YOUR DEATH MATTERS.
A FEW MOMENTS BEFORE, THE MONSTER HAD WORN HER FATHER'S FACE.
AND ELAINE HAD BEEN CRAMMING FOR A PHYSICS EXAM. AND THE WHOLE WORLD MADE SENSE.
LET HER GO! LET HER GO, YOU DEMON!
OH, CHILDREN, THERE IS SO MUCH YOU DON'T KNOW.
BEFORE THERE WERE DEMONS, OR A HELL TO PUT THEM IN, OR A GOD TO CURSE THEM--
--THERE WAS CESTIS--
--OF THE DANCING FLESH.

SORRY ABOUT THIS.
UHH!
CRASSSH
PLAYIN' THROUGH.
CHILDREN'S BODIES SHOULD COME MARKED UP INTO THE DIFFERENT CUTS, LIKE SIRLOIN AND BRISKET.
IT WOULD MAKE CARVING A LOT--
GERRRRONIMO!
NAME'S GAUDIUM, BITCH! SUCK ON IT AND SWALLOW!
Paradiso part 2 of 3
Mike Carey writer • Peter Gross & Ryan Kelly artists
Daniel Vozzo colorist & separations • Comicraft lettering
Christopher Moeller cover painter
Mariah Huehner assistant editor • Shelly Bond editor
Based on characters created by Gaiman, Kieth & Dringenberg

UCK!
CRUNCH
BARRY! SARAH! OH MY GOD!
THERE'S NO TIME FOR THAT BREAST-BEATING SHTICK!
RUN!
MY FRIENDS NEED TO GET TO A HOSPITAL!
THAT THING IS A JIN EN MOK, F'FUCKSAKE!
THEY THROW TRUCKS AT EACH OTHER AS A SIGN OF FRICKIN' AFFECTION!
RRRRRRRRR!
OH LORDY.

IN THE NEVADA DESERT, JILL PRESTO WAS APPROACHING THE GOAL MARKED OUT FOR HER BY THE *BASANOS*.
Rage
THERE. KNEEL DOWN, ON THIS SIDE OF THE GATE.
THE CARDS LOOKED DOWN ON HER WITH FERAL JOY.
AND TAKE OFF THE *SUNGLASSES*.
I CAN'T BELIEVE YOU JUST *KILLED* HIM.
IT WILL HELP YOU TO REMEMBER TO BE *AFRAID* OF US.
NOW LEAN *FORWARD* UNTIL YOUR FACE HAS PASSED THROUGH TO THE FURTHER SIDE.

AT FIRST SHE COULD NOT UNDERSTAND WHAT SHE WAS SEEING.
SKY AND EARTH WERE TWO CAULDRONS--ONE FILLED WITH SMOKE AND FIRE, THE OTHER WITH ROILING DUST.
BUT GRADUALLY SHE REALIZED THAT WHAT SHE WAS SEEING WAS TIME.
THE SKY BOILED AND FLASHED BECAUSE DAYS AND MONTHS WERE GOING BY IN SECONDS.
AND THE FLICKERING LINES DOWN IN THE VALLEY WERE PEOPLE-- LIVING TOO FAST TO SEE.
CABINS GREW BY THE WATERS' EDGE--GREW AND THEN WERE TORN DOWN.
A MINUTE LATER SHE SAW THE FIRST BUILDINGS OF BAKED BRICK.
OUT OF THE HEART OF THE SMALLEST SETTLEMENT, A TOWER ROSE. IT LOOKED LIKE SOMETHING SHE'D SEEN IN A PICTURE ONCE.
IN ITS SHADOW, THE VILLAGE EVOLVED INTO A TOWN. THE TOWN INTO A CITY.
IN LUCIFER'S COSMOS TIME MOVES DIFFERENTLY.
AS LONG AS YOU STAY ON THIS SIDE OF THE GATE, YOU WILL PERCEIVE IT THUS.
WHAT-- WHAT ARE WE DOING HERE?
WAITING.

GAUDIUM, I'VE GOT TO GO BACK! I'VE GOT TO CALL AN AMBULANCE FOR BARRY AND SARAH.
UNDERGROUND
I PUT A TRUCK THROUGH YOUR WALL.
YOU DON'T THINK SOMEONE ELSE MIGHT HAVE NOTICED?
I TOLD YOU--ONE OF THE POWERS IS AFTER YOU. GO BACK AND YOU'RE DEAD.
BUT WHY? IT DOESN'T MAKE ANY SENSE! I'M NOT IMPORTANT.
I AGREE WITH YOU.
WELL, THERE'S THE NOVELTY VALUE.
BUT A TEENAGED ARCHANGEL? I THINK MOST FOLKS WITH ANY TASTE WOULD SAY NO THANKS.
THE THING IS, IT'S THE BASANOS YOU'RE UP AGAINST. IT CAN SEE THE FUTURE.
SO OBVIOUSLY THERE'S A FUTURE WHERE YOU GET TO BE IMPORTANT.
ON THE DOWN SIDE, THERE'S A WHOLE LOT MORE WHERE YOU GET TO BE A GREASY STAIN.
CAN WE TALK AS WE FLEE?

THE WAR COUNCIL OF THE LILIM IN EXILE.
BROTHERS. SISTERS. HEAR ME.
MAZIKEEN, DAUGHTER OF OPHUR, PRESIDES.
GENERAL MISRAN PUT FORTH OUR OFFER TO LUCIFER-- THAT WE WOULD GUARD HIS COSMOS IN EXCHANGE FOR A HOMELAND THERE.
THIS WAS HIS ANSWER.
HE WAS ENTITLED TO REFUSE, BUT THIS--
THIS IS CONTEMPT!
DID HE SAY ANYTHING, MISRAN?
HE SAID THAT WE WERE PLAYING POKER WITHOUT CARDS OR STAKE.
I TAKE THIS TO BE A HUMAN METAPHOR.
HE HAS A MILLION WORLDS. WE ASK ONLY ONE.
WHAT REASON CAN HE HAVE TO REFUSE US?
HIS CURSED PRIDE IS ALL THE REASON HE NEEDS. HE DOES AS HE LIKES.

GONE BEGGING FOR FAVORS AND IT DID NOT SERVE.
I PROPOSE WE TAKE WHAT WE NEED, AND PRESENT LUCIFER WITH A FAIT ACCOMPLI.
FORCES MAZIKEEN HAS RECRUITED FROM HELL, WE ARE A STRONGER POWER THAN BEFORE.
BUT TO GO AGAINST LUCIFER...IS IT POSSIBLE?
I WOULD NOT RECOMMEND IT. THE COST WOULD BE HIGH.
BUT IT IS MY PLACE TO ENFORCE THE WILL OF THIS ASSEMBLY. AMELECH HAS PROPOSED AND YOU MUST VOTE.
TWO HAVE ABSTAINED. TEN HAVE SPOKEN.
THE VOTE IS IN FAVOR OF WAR AGAINST LUCIFER MORNINGSTAR.

WHEN SHE HAD BEEN WATCHING FOR ALMOST AN *HOUR*, THE FIRST SKYSCRAPERS WENT UP.
AS FAR AS SHE COULD TELL, THEY WERE MADE MOSTLY OF BLACK VOLCANIC GLASS. RAINBOW LIGHT PLAYED ABOUT THEIR PINNACLES.
ROADS UNROLLED ACROSS THE DESERT FLOOR, CROSSING AND RECROSSING UNTIL THERE WAS NO DESERT LEFT.

IF SHE LEANED FORWARD AND SQUINTED HER EYES, THE FLOW OF TIME SLOWED, AND SHE COULD SEE CHARIOTS OF STRANGE DESIGN THAT TRAVELED THOSE ROADS.
AND THE SKIES FILLED UP WITH THE PAINTED CANOPIES OF AIRSHIPS, WITH SLENDER SKY-PLATFORMS SUSPENDED BY MEANS SHE COULD NOT GUESS.
THE STRANGE SHRILL WHISPER THAT WASHED OVER HER WAS MUSIC, ACCELERATED PAST ANY PITCH HER EARS COULD TRANSLATE.
THE AIR WAS RIPE WITH PERFUMES FROM GARDENS AND ARBORETA, AND THE RAINBOWS RAN DOWN THE STREETS LIKE RIVERS, IN AN ENDLESS HYMN OF LIGHT.
AND SOMETHING INSIDE HER FILLED WITH LONGING, SO THAT SHE STOOD AND STEPPED FORWARD THROUGH THE GATE.
SHE WANTED--WANTED MORE THAN ANYTHING--TO MEET THE PEOPLE WHO HAD BROUGHT FORTH SUCH BEAUTY...

DON'T GET TOO ATTACHED TO ANYTHING YOU SEE.
WHAT? YOU MEAN--?
NONE OF IT IS GOING TO LAST.
SHIT! I DON'T WANT TO STAND HERE AND WATCH A REAL-LIFE DISASTER MOVIE.
CAN'T WE WARN THEM?
NO. YOU MISUNDERSTAND.
WHEN WE RULE HERE, EVERYTHING WILL CHANGE. WE WILL NEED ROOM TO LIVE IN.
THE HOUR IS ALMOST UPON US. WHEN HE LOOKS AWAY, ALL THINGS WILL HANG UPON THE CUSP.
"ROOM TO LIVE IN"? WHAT ARE YOU TALKING ABOUT?
THAT'S A WHOLE FUCKING UNIVERSE OUT THERE!
THAT'S WHY WE CAME, JILL.
THAT'S EXACTLY WHAT WE WERE LOOKING FOR.

THIS... IS...NO GOOD!
WHAT? WHY? WHAT ARE YOU DOING?
I CAN'T... GO ANY FURTHER.
JUST NEED TO GET MY BREATH BACK.
BUT SHE'S RIGHT BEHIND YOU!
NO.
SHE'S RIGHT IN FRONT OF YOU.
THAT'S MORE SATISFYING SOMEHOW, ISN'T IT?

OOH! QUICK AND SLICK. LIKE IT.
BUT IF WINGS ARE YOUR BIG THING--

--THEN A HOLE IN THE GROUND WAS A STUPID PLACE TO HIDE.
EEEYAAARGHHH!

AARGH! GONNA EAT YOUR FUCKIN' EYEBALLS, YOU RABID JIN EN MOK BITCH!
YOU TOUCH THE KID, YOU ANSWER TO ME!
FSSSST!

SKLUP

YOU KNOW, THIS WASN'T MUCH FUN--EITHER AS A HUNT OR A FIGHT.
BUT THAT'S WHAT HAPPENS. YOU START TAKING ON COMMISSIONS AND THE QUALITY OF YOUR WORK GOES ALL TO SHIT.
TO BE HONEST, I DON'T EVEN FEEL MUCH LIKE EATING YOU.
YOU SMELL OF HEAVEN. I HATE THAT.
SO LET'S GO FOR A SIMPLE FUNERAL. NO FLOWERS OR KNOWN GRASSES.
CHOOM
IT'S WHAT YOUR DADDY WOULD HAVE WANTED.
FOOM

Lux
I'D LIKE TO HAVE A WORD WITH YOU, IF IT'S NOT TOO MUCH TROUBLE.
CRASHH
COME OUT AND TALK TO ME!
YOU OWE ME THAT MUCH!

WE OWE EACH OTHER NOTHING.
IF I'D INCURRED A DEBT, BELIEVE ME, I WOULD HAVE REMEMBERED.
THE LILIM HAVE VOTED FOR WAR.
AGAINST YOU.
I KNOW. I AM PREPARED FOR WAR.
I LOST MY FACE IN YOUR SERVICE. AND YOU'VE OPENED THE DOORS TO EVERYONE ELSE.
ALL THEY ARE ASKING FOR IS A REALM OF THEIR OWN.
AND WHAT ARE THEY OFFERING?
YOU KNOW WHAT THEY'RE OFFERING. THEIR SERVICE WHEN YOU NEED THEM.
HMM. AND THERE'S THE RUB, OF COURSE. I DON'T NEED ANYONE.
NOW IS THIS REALLY ABOUT TERRITORY?
OR IS IT ABOUT YOU AND ME?

NOW.

SHALL WE WALK, OR SHALL WE RIDE?
RIDE. THEY MUST SEE US IN OUR GLORY AND MAJESTY.

COME, JILL PRESTO. YOU'LL BE WITH US IN OUR TRIUMPH.
THIS IS THE SEVENTEENTH TRUMP.

THE *CHARIOT.*

COULD WE BE ANY *MORE* CONSPICUOUS?

PERHAPS. A LITTLE.

WE'RE NOT *BURGLARS,* JILL.

WE'RE *CONQUERORS.*

GOOD DAY TO YOU, STRANGERS.

AND TO YOU.

YOU ARE MOST *ODDLY* CONVEYED.

WE ARE THE BASANOS. OUR CHARIOT IS *OURSELF*.
ARE WE NOT *BEAUTIFUL*, MORTAL MAN?

YOU ARE...STRIKING, CERTAINLY. BUT WHAT'S YOUR PURPOSE HERE?
TO *FULFILL* YOU. TO BRING YOU WHAT YOU HAVE *CRAVED* FOR ALL THESE GENERATIONS.

CHILDREN OF LUCIFER, YOU HAVE *REAL* GODS NOW.
BOW DOWN.

YOU I WILL ALLOW. BUT MY WORLD HAS NO HEAVEN NOR HELL.
I'VE NO INTENTION OF IMPORTING THEM.
THE LILIM BELONG TO NEITHER. GIVE THEM WHAT THEY ASK AND THEY'LL SWEAR FEALTY TO YOU.

OF COURSE THEY WILL.
AND THEN THEY'LL SPLIT INTO A DOZEN FACTIONS AND ARGUE ABOUT THE SMALL PRINT FOREVER.
THEY WHINE EVEN AS THEY BITE. LIKE DOGS.

AS YOU WILL, THEN. TAKE THIS AS A DECLARATION OF WAR.
IT'S MORE NOTICE THAN I EXPECTED, TO BE HONEST. BUT LET'S BE CLEAR ABOUT--
...

SOMETHING ELSE HAS COME UP.
MY OFFER STANDS. COME ALONE AND YOU'LL BE WELCOME.

I TRIED THAT.
IT DIDN'T WORK.

OH JESUS, I AM IN SUCH DEEP SHIT.
DEEP DEEP DEEP DEEP DEEP.
HE'S GONNA BLAME ME FOR THIS.
THERE IS NO WAY HE'S GONNA LISTEN TO MY VERSION. OH NO.
GAUDIUM!
GAAAAAAAAH! IT WASN'T MY FAULT!
IF YOU WOULD'VE RUN WHEN I FIRST ASKED YOU, YOU WOULDN'T HAVE DIED!
I'M NOT DEAD--I'M SPIRIT WALKING. I THINK ANGELS MUST BE REALLY HARD TO KILL.
COME ON.
WELL, YOU KNOW WE COULD JUST COWER DOWN HERE IN THE DARK FOR AWHILE...
NO. WE'RE GOING TO FIND LUCIFER.
HE'LL KNOW WHAT TO DO.
To Be Continued...

SSSSSS
OMMMMMME
WE DON'T WORSHIP. WE'RE FORBIDDEN TO.
THERE ARE NO GODS HERE.
BUT THERE ARE. WE ARE GODS.
THINNNNNNNNGGG
IF YOU'RE GODS, THEN I'VE NO WISH TO OFFEND.
BUT I CAN'T BOW DOWN TO YOU. I'M SORRY.
ELLLLLLSSSSSSSE
HHHHHHASSSSSS
WELL, WE WILL HAVE YOU ON YOUR KNEES ONE WAY OR ANOTHER, MAN.
FOR YOUR SAKE, YOU MIGHT HAVE CHOSEN THE EASIER ROAD.
AS I SAID, I'M SORRY.
COMMMMMMME
UPPPPPPPPPP.
DON'T BE SORRY.
WE LIKE IT JUST AS MUCH THIS WAY.

THE BASANOS WAS MEANT TO MIMIC DESTINY'S BOOK, THE ULTIMATE TOOL OF DIVINATION.
BUT THE DESIGN WAS *FLAWED*.
IT ISN'T CLEAR, EVEN TO ME, HOW IT *REALLY* FUNCTIONS.
IT IS *ALIVE* NOW. AND ITS EXQUISITE SENSES CAN SNIFF OUT THE *FULCRA* OF HUMAN WILL AND PHYSICAL SYSTEMS.
THE MOMENTS AND THE MOLECULES ON WHICH THE *FUTURE* BALANCES.
I SUPPOSE THERE WAS A VOLCANIC CALDERA UNDERNEATH THE CITY.

I SUPPOSE THERE WAS A MEASURABLE CHANCE THAT IT WOULD *ERUPT*.
AND SO IT DID.
Paradiso
part 3 of 3
Mike Carey writer • Peter Gross & Ryan Kelly artists
Daniel Vozzo colorist & separations • Comicraft lettering
Christopher Moeller cover painter
Mariah Huehner assistant editor • Shelly Bond editor
Based on characters created by Gaiman, Kieth & Dringenberg

THE PROBLEM WAS *TIME.*
NOT THE TIME IT TOOK HIM TO ASSIMILATE AND RESPOND.
THAT WAS AS NEAR AS POSSIBLE TO BEING *INSTANTANEOUS.*
AND NOT THE TIME IT TOOK HIM TO *MOVE.*
HE COULD HAVE CIRCLED THE *EARTH,* IF HE CHOSE TO, BEFORE HIS IMAGE FADED FROM MAZIKEEN'S EYE.
BUT THE *GRADIENT* OF TIME WAS AGAINST HIM.
THE GRADIENT HE HIMSELF HAD SET, WHEN HE WAS *BUILDING* HIS UNIVERSE FROM THE RAW MATERIALS OF THE VOID.
HE WOULD BE THERE IN A *HEARTBEAT.*
BUT WHILE A HEART MIGHT BEAT ONCE ON *THIS* SIDE OF THE GATE--
--ON THE FAR SIDE THE SUN MIGHT RISE--
--AND *SET.*

AND THE SUN LOOKED AWAY.
AND NO HELP CAME.
SHIT! I CAN'T STAND HERE AND WATCH THIS.
I JUST CAN'T!
WELL, JILL--
--WE HAVE NO OBJECTION TO YOU CLOSING YOUR EYES.
BASANOS, I...I UNDERSTAND YOUR POWER A LITTLE BETTER NOW. I BOW TO YOU.
OF COURSE YOU DO.
AND I BEG YOU TO STOP THIS.
AH, BUT THAT'S NOT SO EASY.
WE PUSH THE PEBBLE THAT STARTS THE AVALANCHE.
BUT WHERE IS THE PEBBLE THAT WILL MAKE THE AVALANCHE FORBEAR?

LONDON.

FRIGGIN' VICTORIAN CIVIC *ARCHITECTURE.*

THERE'S NO FRIGGIN' *HANDLE* ON THIS THING! NOTHIN'!

CHOOOOM

NO SIGN OF THE *BITCH* QUEEN. YOU CAN COME ON UP ELAINE.

I'LL NEVER PLAY THE *PIANO* AGAIN, BUT THAT'S ALL PART OF THE --
FINE. YOU'RE *WELCOME.* THIS JOB SUCKS THE BIG VEINY ONE, Y'KNOW?
BODYGUARD TO A KID WHO HASN'T EVEN *GOT* A BODY ANYMORE. DO *YOU* SEE ANY SENSE IN THAT?

BUT I NEVER ASKED YOU TO BE MY BODYGUARD. AND I DON'T BELIEVE LUCIFER DID EITHER.
YOU'VE GOT YOUR OWN REASONS FOR STAYING CLOSE TO ME.
DON'T POINT. IT'S OFFENSIVE.

OKAY, MAYBE I COULD'VE BEEN A BIT MORE UP-FRONT ABOUT A COUPLE OF THINGS.
BUT I SAVED YOUR LIFE, REMEMBER? THAT ENTITLES ME TO SOME PRIVACY.

UH... I DID SAVE YOUR LIFE, RIGHT?
I SUPPOSE.
ONLY WE LEFT YOUR BODY LYIN' UNDER A GIRDER BACK THERE AND NOW HERE WE ARE IN A CEMETERY. IT DON'T LOOK TOO GOOD.

I TOLD YOU, GAUDIUM. WE'RE LOOKING FOR LUCIFER.
RIGHT. GOT YOU. AND THIS IS EXACTLY THE KIND OF PLACE WHERE HE TENDS TO--

OH. YEAH.
I GUESS THERE IS THAT.

THE HOUSE OF WINDOWLESS ROOMS.

SUSANO-O-NO-MIKOTO CLIMBED TO HIS FEET.
HE WAS WEAK FROM FASTING. DRAINED AND DIZZY FROM THE INTENSITY OF HIS MEDITATION. BUT HIS MIND WAS A CLAW CLOSED AROUND A SINGLE THOUGHT.
LUCIFER.

HE TOOK THREE STEPS TOWARDS THE BRAZIER.
FORBIDDEN TO HELP HIM, OR EVEN SPEAK, THE SERVANTS MERELY WATCHED.
AND THE TANG OF WHITE-HOT METAL CURDLED THE AIR.

YOU BASTARDS! YOU KNEW THIS WOULD HAPPEN.
NO. NOT ALL.
THAT WHICH TOUCHES OUR OWN FUTURE SELDOM COMES ENTIRELY CLEAR.
OH.
RIGHT.
WELL MAYBE IT'S JUST A MATTER OF FOCUS...
AHHRRRR!

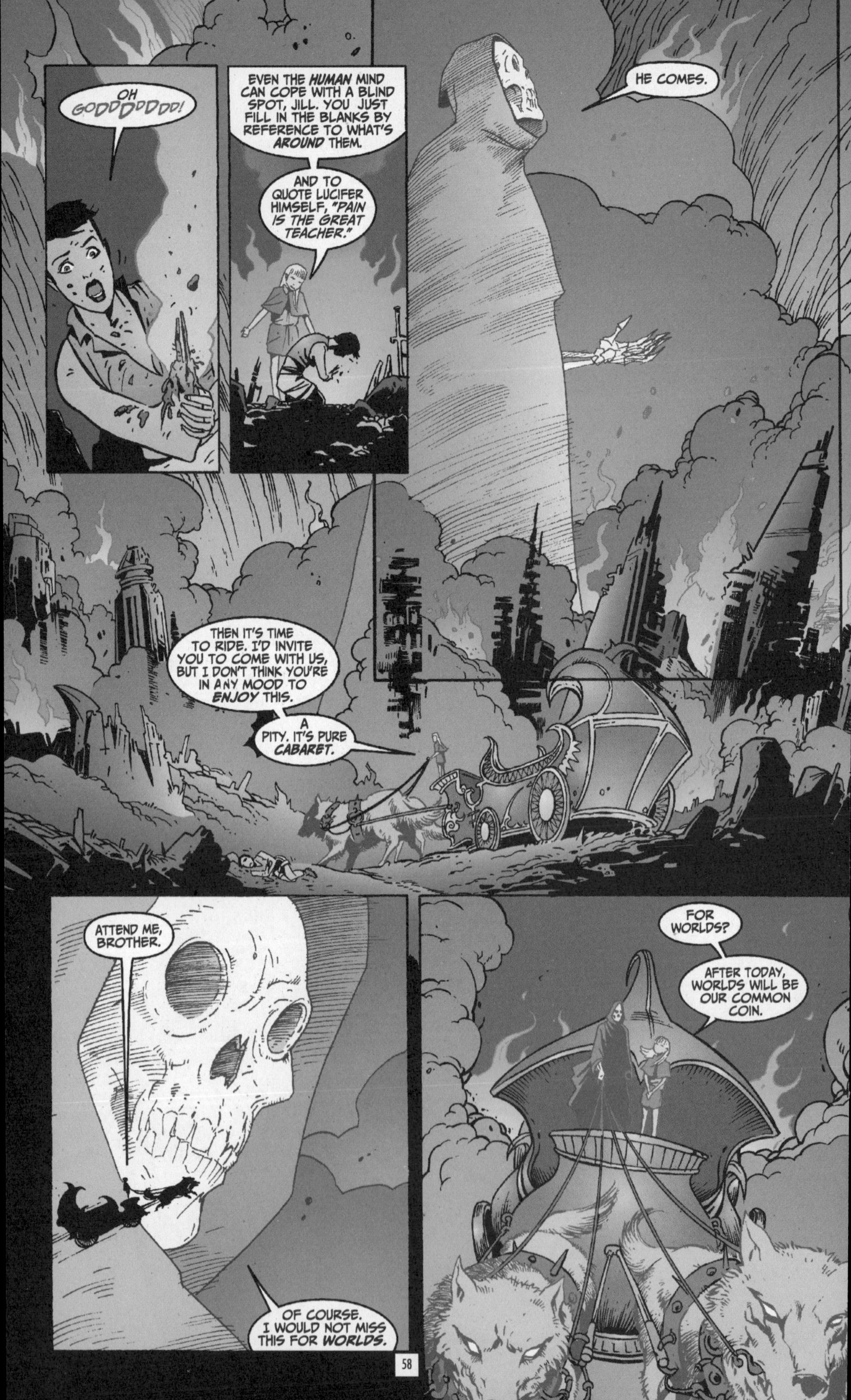
OH GODDDDDDD!
EVEN THE HUMAN MIND CAN COPE WITH A BLIND SPOT, JILL. YOU JUST FILL IN THE BLANKS BY REFERENCE TO WHAT'S AROUND THEM.
AND TO QUOTE LUCIFER HIMSELF, "PAIN IS THE GREAT TEACHER."
HE COMES.
THEN IT'S TIME TO RIDE. I'D INVITE YOU TO COME WITH US, BUT I DON'T THINK YOU'RE IN ANY MOOD TO ENJOY THIS.
A PITY. IT'S PURE CABARET.
ATTEND ME, BROTHER.
OF COURSE. I WOULD NOT MISS THIS FOR WORLDS.
FOR WORLDS?
AFTER TODAY, WORLDS WILL BE OUR COMMON COIN.

THE TANG OF WHITE-HOT METAL CURDLED THE AIR.
ONE OF THE *DOVES* PECKED AT THE BARS OF ITS CAGE-- A SOUND THAT JARRED BY ITS VERY INNOCENCE.
SUSANO STOOD BEFORE THE BRAZIER. ITS HEAT DID NOT SEEM TO *RADIATE*.
RATHER IT *SUCKED* AT HIM LIKE SOME HELLISH UNDERTOW.
IT PULLED HIS HANDS *FORWARD*.
PERHAPS HE *FOUGHT* FOR A MOMENT, BUT IT MADE NO DIFFERENCE NOW.
THE *FIRE* WOULD HAVE ITS WAY.
SKIN BLISTERED.
BLOOD BOILED.
FLESH FLAKED.
TORTURED METAL *ADHERED* TO BARE BONE.
HHHHHH!

IT IS STRANGE TO EXPERIENCE AT LAST THE MOMENT WE HAVE SO OFTEN FORESEEN.
IS IT STRANGE? ALL MOMENTS ARE ONE MOMENT, SURELY?
EXCEPT FOR THOSE ON WHICH OUR OWN DESTINY HANGS.
THOSE ARE STRANGE INDEED. AND FRIGHTENING.
WILL YOU SPEAK WITH US BEFORE YOU STRIKE, MORNINGSTAR?
THERE'S NOTHING TO SAY.

WHERE ARE WE?
OH WHERE DO YOU THINK? HIS PLACE. HIS WORLD.
DON'T RUB MY FRIGGIN' NOSE IN IT, OKAY?
GAUDIUM.. IS THAT--?
I'M KEEPIN' OUTTA THIS, OKAY?
FAR AS I'M CONCERNED, IT'S NOT HAPPENING.
DUM DEE DUM. NICE DAY. I DON'T SEEEE ANYTHING.

LUCIFER, YOU KNOW NOTHING OF OUR POWER.
AND I CARE NOTHING FOR IT.
I SHOULD HAVE DEALT WITH YOU IN HAMBURG, BASANOS. BUT I SUPPOSE YOUR BREATH WAS ON THE DICE.
YOU TOUCHED WHAT WAS MINE.
YOU CHOSE THIS DEATH.

NOW!
DO IT NOW!

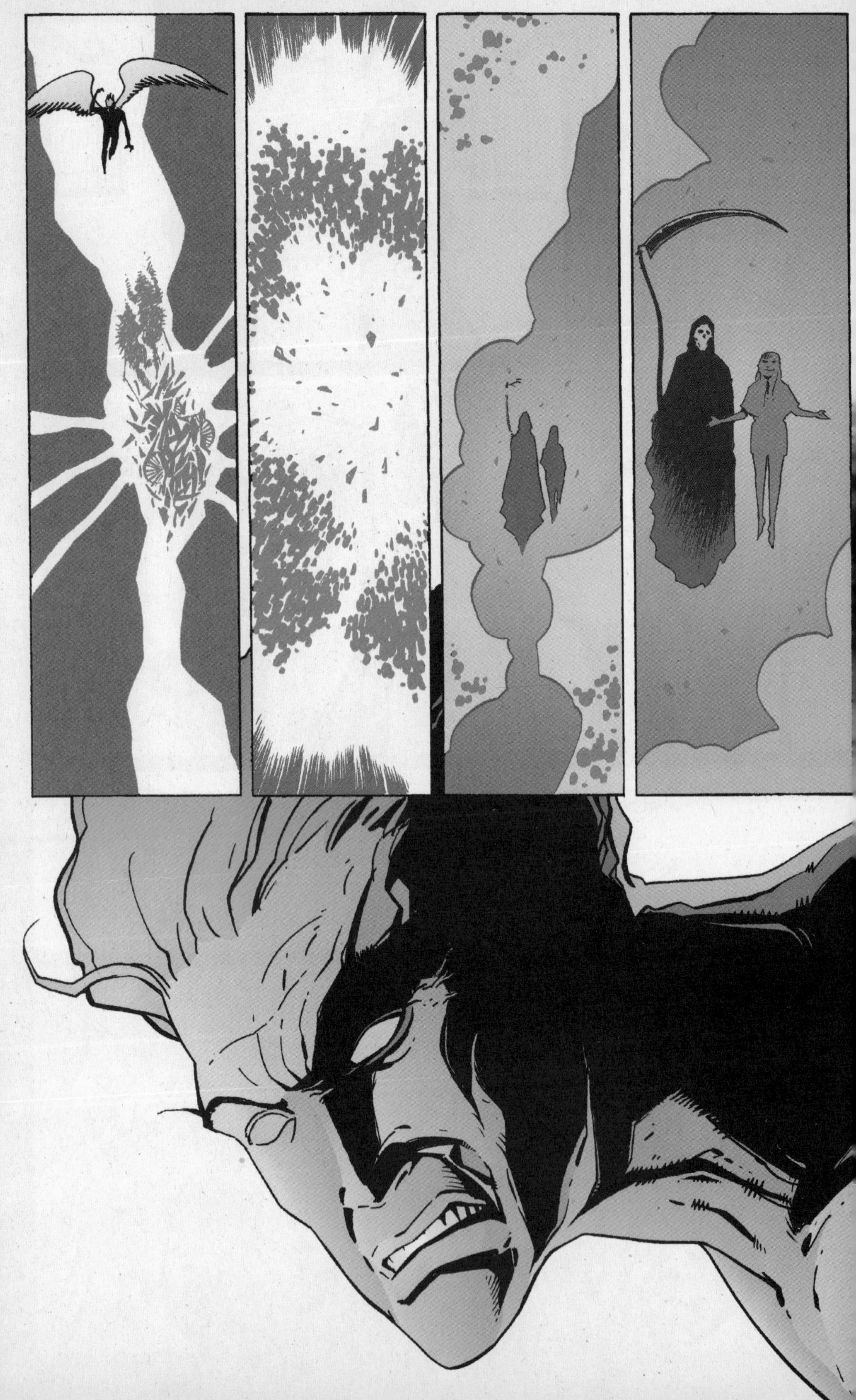

YOU SEE IT NOW. AS WE SAW IT TWO YEARS AGO.
WHEN YOU COMMANDED US TO FORETELL YOUR FUTURE. WHEN WE REALIZED FOR THE FIRST TIME THAT YOU COULD BE DEFEATED.
"THE POWER YOU SUMMONED TO DESTROY US IS STILL INSIDE YOU. HELD THERE BY THE FEATHERS THAT IZANAMI WOVE INTO YOUR WINGS."
A GREAT MAGIC, MORNINGSTAR, AND VERY SLOW IN THE WEAVING.
NOT AS GREAT AS THE FORCES AT YOUR DISPOSAL, OF COURSE. BUT THEN THAT'S THE POINT.
WHEN YOU RAISE YOUR HAND TO STRIKE, THE STARS THEMSELVES DIM.
SO HOW LONG WILL YOU BE ABLE TO BALANCE THOSE FORCES WITHIN YOURSELF--
--BEFORE THEY CONSUME YOU?

EEEEaaaRRRRGGGhhhhhh!

WELL, THAT'S *THAT*, I GUESS.
NOTHING MUCH *WE* CAN --

DON'T *DO* THIS, KID! DON'T DRAW *ATTENTION* TO YOURSELF!

THEY'LL RIP YOU *APART*!

FOR THE PISSING, PUKING LOVE O' GOD, YOU'RE JUST A *SPIRIT*!
WHAT DO YOU THINK YOU'RE GONNA DO?

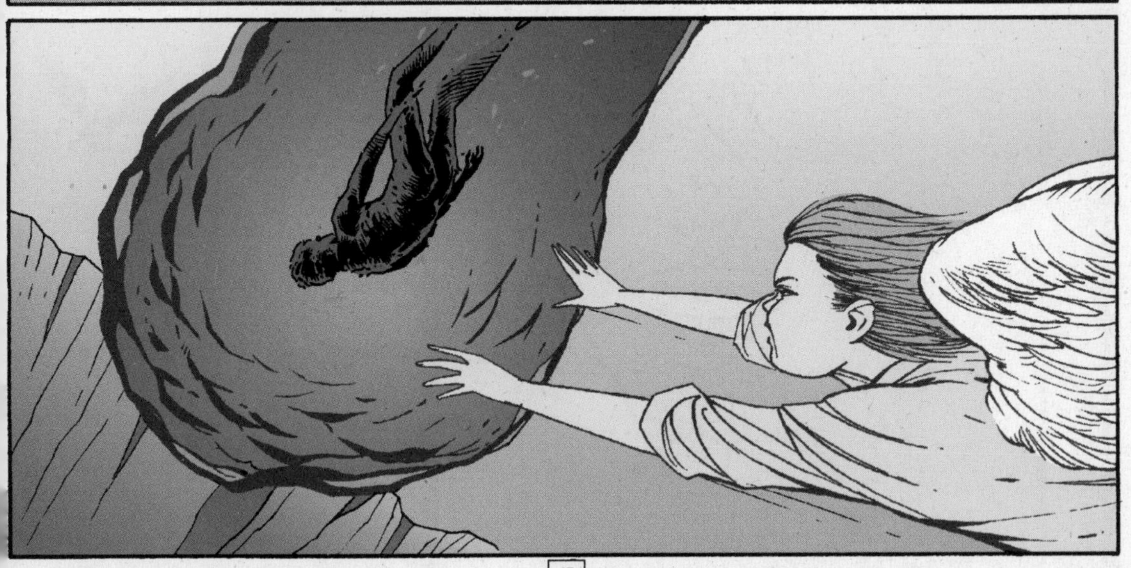

UHHHH!
THE HALF ANGEL! OUR ASSASSIN MISCARRIED.
IT DOESN'T MATTER. SHE'S TOO LATE.
THE OUTCOME IS CERTAIN NOW.
NNNNNNG!
NO!
NO!
NO!

"IT CAME TO NOTHING. THESE THINGS NEVER DO."
"I MAKE MY OWN CHOICES. AS YOU'VE DONE."
"AS EVERYBODY DOES."
"BUT IT MATTERS NOT. I HAVE HAD MY FILL OF THE OLD LIFE."
"THERE'S ALWAYS THE ULTIMATE FREEDOM."
"YOU DON'T HAVE TO STAY ANYWHERE FOREVER."
"DID YOU THINK FIRE WOULD BURN ME?"
"I'M THE LIGHTBRINGER. THE SHEPHERD OF SUNS."
"AS IF MERELY SAYING SOMETHING WERE ENOUGH TO MAKE IT TRUE."

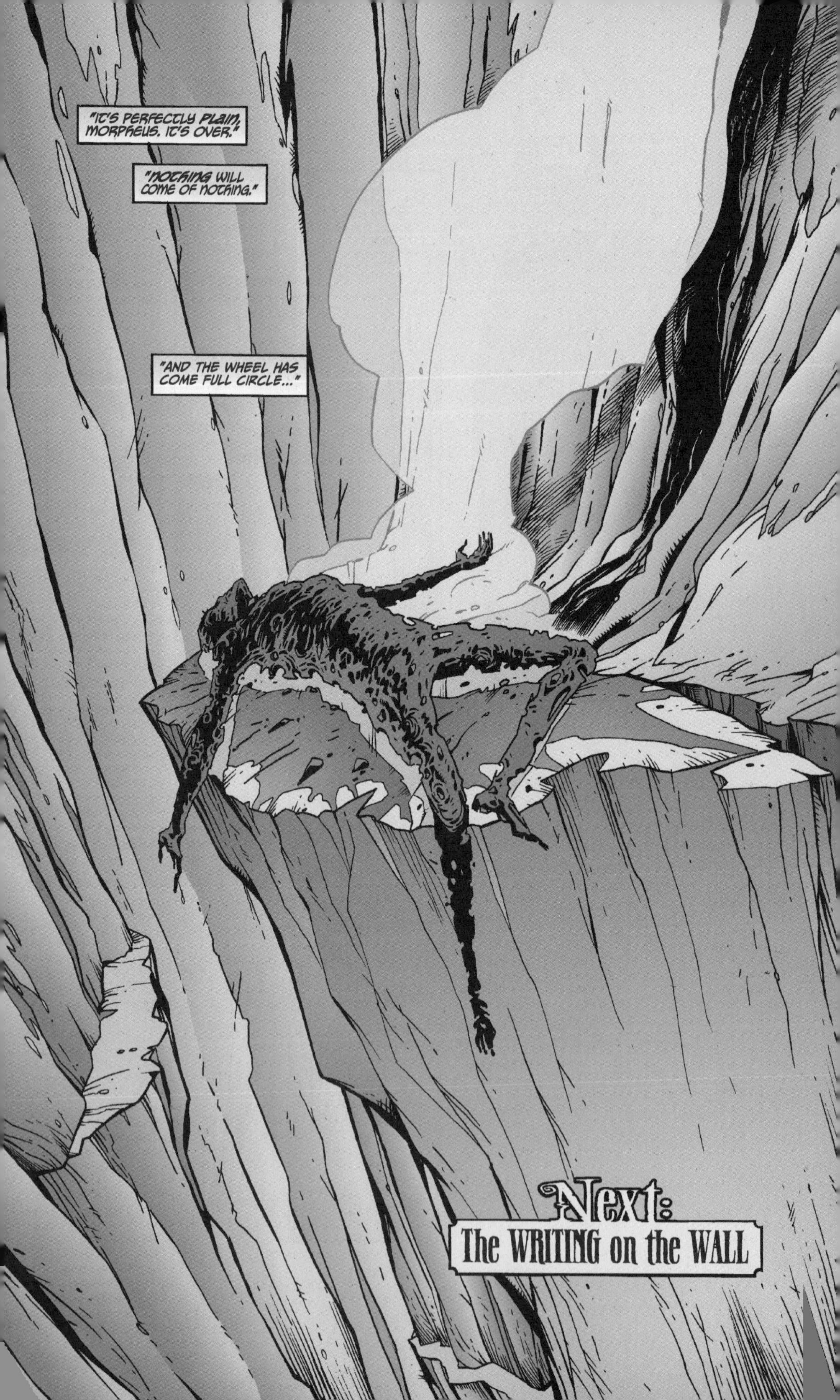
"IT'S PERFECTLY PLAIN, MORPHEUS. IT'S OVER."
"NOTHING WILL COME OF NOTHING."
"AND THE WHEEL HAS COME FULL CIRCLE..."
Next:
The WRITING on the WALL

The Writing on the Wall
WARS ARE WON AND LOST BY COMMUNICATION, MY MOTHER SAID.
OBVIOUSLY SO, WHEN VAST NUMBERS MARCH ACROSS WHOLE CONTINENTS. BUT JUST AS TRULY IN SMALL SKIRMISHES TOO.
WHEN THE TWO-LEGS CAME FROM IBLIS TO TAKE OUR LANDS, MY MOTHER WENT OUT ALONE TO MEET THEM.
SHE WAS ALLOWED TO DO SO BECAUSE SHE WAS ESA-HANE, THE SORCERESS. AND SHE HAD SAID THAT IT WOULD BE SO.
SHE ASKED THE LEADER OF THE TWO-LEGS WHAT IT WAS THAT HE DESIRED MORE THAN ALL ELSE.
HE THOUGHT FOR A MOMENT AND THEN SAID "POWER."
SO SHE DREW OFF A LITTLE OF THE SUN, AND MADE IT DANCE ABOVE HIS HEAD.
"SEE, HERE IS POWER," SHE SAID TO HIM.
"REACH UP AND TAKE IT, OH MAN. OR SHALL I BRING IT DOWN FOR YOU?"
AND THE TWO-LEGS WENT HOME TO IBLIS.
SHE WAS A GOOD COMMUNICATOR, MY MOTHER. SHE DID NOT WASTE WORDS. BUT AS FOR ME--
--ALL MY LIFE I HAVE DONE NOTHING ELSE.

MIKE CAREY WRITER • DEAN ORMSTON ARTIST • COMICRAFT LETTERING • DANIEL VOZZO COLORIST & SEPARATOR
CHRISTOPHER MOELLER COVER PAINTER • MARIAH HUEHNER ASSISTANT EDITOR • SHELLY BOND EDITOR

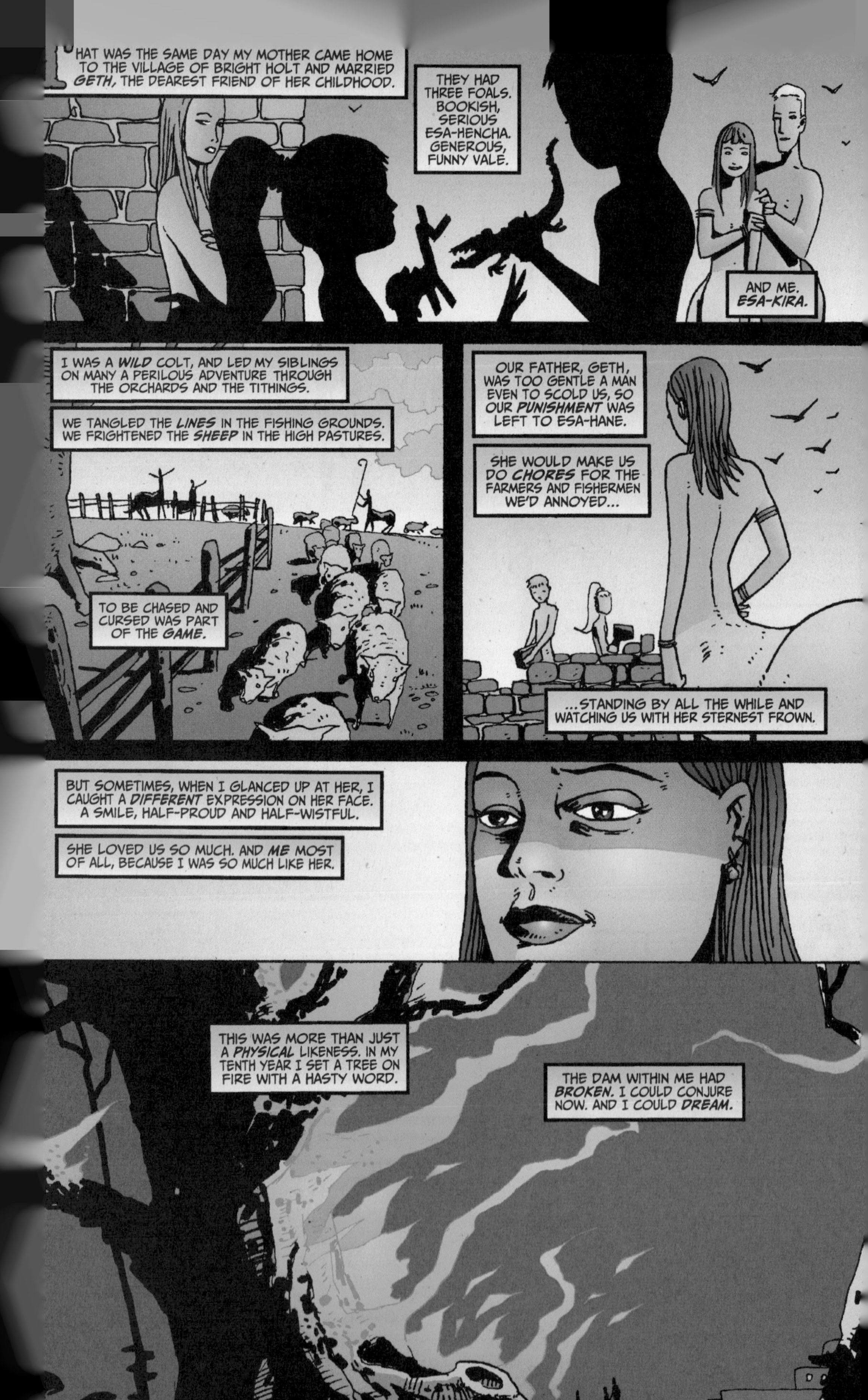
THAT WAS THE SAME DAY MY MOTHER CAME HOME TO THE VILLAGE OF BRIGHT HOLT AND MARRIED *GETH,* THE DEAREST FRIEND OF HER CHILDHOOD.
THEY HAD THREE FOALS. BOOKISH, SERIOUS ESA-HENCHA. GENEROUS, FUNNY VALE.
AND ME. *ESA-KIRA.*
I WAS A *WILD* COLT, AND LED MY SIBLINGS ON MANY A PERILOUS ADVENTURE THROUGH THE ORCHARDS AND THE TITHINGS.
WE TANGLED THE *LINES* IN THE FISHING GROUNDS. WE FRIGHTENED THE *SHEEP* IN THE HIGH PASTURES.
TO BE CHASED AND CURSED WAS PART OF THE *GAME.*
OUR FATHER, GETH, WAS TOO GENTLE A MAN EVEN TO SCOLD US, SO OUR *PUNISHMENT* WAS LEFT TO ESA-HANE.
SHE WOULD MAKE US DO *CHORES* FOR THE FARMERS AND FISHERMEN WE'D ANNOYED...
...STANDING BY ALL THE WHILE AND WATCHING US WITH HER STERNEST FROWN.
BUT SOMETIMES, WHEN I GLANCED UP AT HER, I CAUGHT A *DIFFERENT* EXPRESSION ON HER FACE. A SMILE, HALF-PROUD AND HALF-WISTFUL.
SHE LOVED US SO MUCH. AND *ME* MOST OF ALL, BECAUSE I WAS SO MUCH LIKE HER.
THIS WAS MORE THAN JUST A *PHYSICAL* LIKENESS. IN MY TENTH YEAR I SET A TREE ON FIRE WITH A HASTY WORD.
THE DAM WITHIN ME HAD *BROKEN.* I COULD CONJURE NOW. AND I COULD *DREAM.*

ONE CHILD INHERITS THE SIGHT AND THE SPARK. I THOUGHT IT WOULD BE HENCHA, BUT THE STARS SAID OTHERWISE.
AND VALE IS A BOY, OF COURSE.
BUT, MOTHER, THE DREAMS ARE ABOUT WAR. A WAR THAT WILL SWALLOW UP THE WORLD.

THERE WILL ALWAYS BE WARS, KI. JUST AS THERE WILL ALWAYS BE STORMS.
AND THEN THE SUN COMES OUT AGAIN AND THE PUDDLES DRY. LIFE IS STRONGER THAN DEATH.

IN MY DREAMS... I SAW THE MAKER FALL. STRUCK DOWN IN BATTLE.
I THINK I SAW HIM DIE.

WE'LL TALK ABOUT THIS ANOTHER TIME. COME.
YOU'RE A SORCERESS NOW. THERE ARE THINGS THAT MUST BE ARRANGED.
SHE TOOK ME OUT OF THE VILLAGE SCHOOL SO SHE COULD UNDERTAKE MY EDUCATION HERSELF.

IN THE YEAR THAT FOLLOWED SHE FANNED THE SPARK OF MAGIC INSIDE ME INTO A SMALL, BRIGHT FLAME.
AND THEN SHE BEGAN TO TEACH ME HOW TO DRAW ON ITS HEAT AND ITS POWER.

BUT AT NIGHT THE DREAMS WOULD COME MORE AND MORE VIVIDLY.
MAKING SLEEP IMPOSSIBLE.

THE MAKER IN HIS WRATH AND HIS MAJESTY, ASSAILING THE *CHARIOT* OF HIS FOES.

AND THEN STRUCK DOWN *HIMSELF* BY A MAGICAL ATTACK FROM BEHIND.

HIS BODY BURNING AND FALLING. HIS *SCREAM* IN MY MIND LIKE A RAIN OF GLASS SPLINTERS.

MOTHER, WHAT SHOULD I *DO?* THE MAKER NEEDS TO BE WARNED. HE MAY NOT KNOW HE IS IN DANGER!
KI...
IN *MY* DREAMS THE MAKER APPEARS AS A ROCK. WHAT DOES THAT MEAN?
UMM... THAT HE'S THE *FOUNDATION* OF OUR WORLD AND OUR LIFE?
THAT HE'S THE ONLY THING WE CAN *DEPEND* ON?

NO, FOR HE WAS A ROCK IN SHALLOW *WATERS,* WHERE GREAT SHIPS PASSED.
THERE ARE ROCKS ON WHICH YOU *BUILD,* KI, AND THERE ARE ROCKS ON WHICH YOU *BREAK.*
SHE CRIED THEN. AND I DIDN'T KNOW WHY.

IDIOT.
I WAS HER *DAUGHTER*--HER SECOND SELF. SHE DIDN'T NEED THE SIGHT OR THE SPARK TO KNOW WHAT WAS IN MY MIND.

I WAS *THIRTEEN* YEARS OLD. THERE WAS A BOY CALLED ENU IN BIRCH FASTNESS WHO HAD ASKED FOR MY HAND, BUT MOTHER SAID I WAS TOO YOUNG.
TOO YOUNG! THE NEXT MORNING I ROSE WITH THE SUN.
AND SET OFF THROUGH THE DEW AND THE THOUSANDFOLD BIRDSONG TO *SAVE* THE MAKER.

I HAD A *PLAN*. IT DEPENDED ON THE GATES.
ALL THE FOLK KNOW OF THEM, AND THAT THEY ARE *DOORWAYS* TO OTHER WORLDS.
FOR THE MOST PART WE *AVOID* THEM. FOR WHO WOULD WANT MORE THAN THE MAKER HAS GIVEN US?
BUT IN THE ISLANDS OF THE *SOUTH*, SAILORS SAID, THERE IS A GATE A HUNDRED HANDS HIGH, WHICH OPENS TO A *PALACE* OF WHITE MARBLE.
THIS MUST BE THE MAKER'S HOUSE, I REASONED. FOR THE GREATEST *DOOR* MUST LEAD TO THE GREATEST *DESTINATION*.
STAY CLEAR OF THE *ROPES*, MISSY. YOU GET A TANGLE OF THAT AROUND YOUR LEG, YOU'LL *BREAK* IT FOR SURE.
OH! THANK YOU.
EVERYONE I ASKED SAID THAT THE SWEET WIND WAS GOING SOUTH THAT SAME DAY. I SLIPPED ON BOARD, UNSEEN, AND FOUND A PLACE IN THE HOLD, BEHIND SOME BOLTS OF CLOTH.
IN THE EVENING SHE SET SAIL.
AND IN THE FIRST ROUGH *SEA*, WHEN THE CREWMEN CAME TO TIE THE CARGO DOWN, THEY FOUND ME THERE, *GREEN* AND GROANING.
THE FIRST MATE WAS FOR PUTTING ME DOWN IN THE DORY BOAT AND LETTING ME MAKE MY OWN WAY HOME. BUT THE CAPTAIN SAID I'D *WORK* MY PASSAGE.

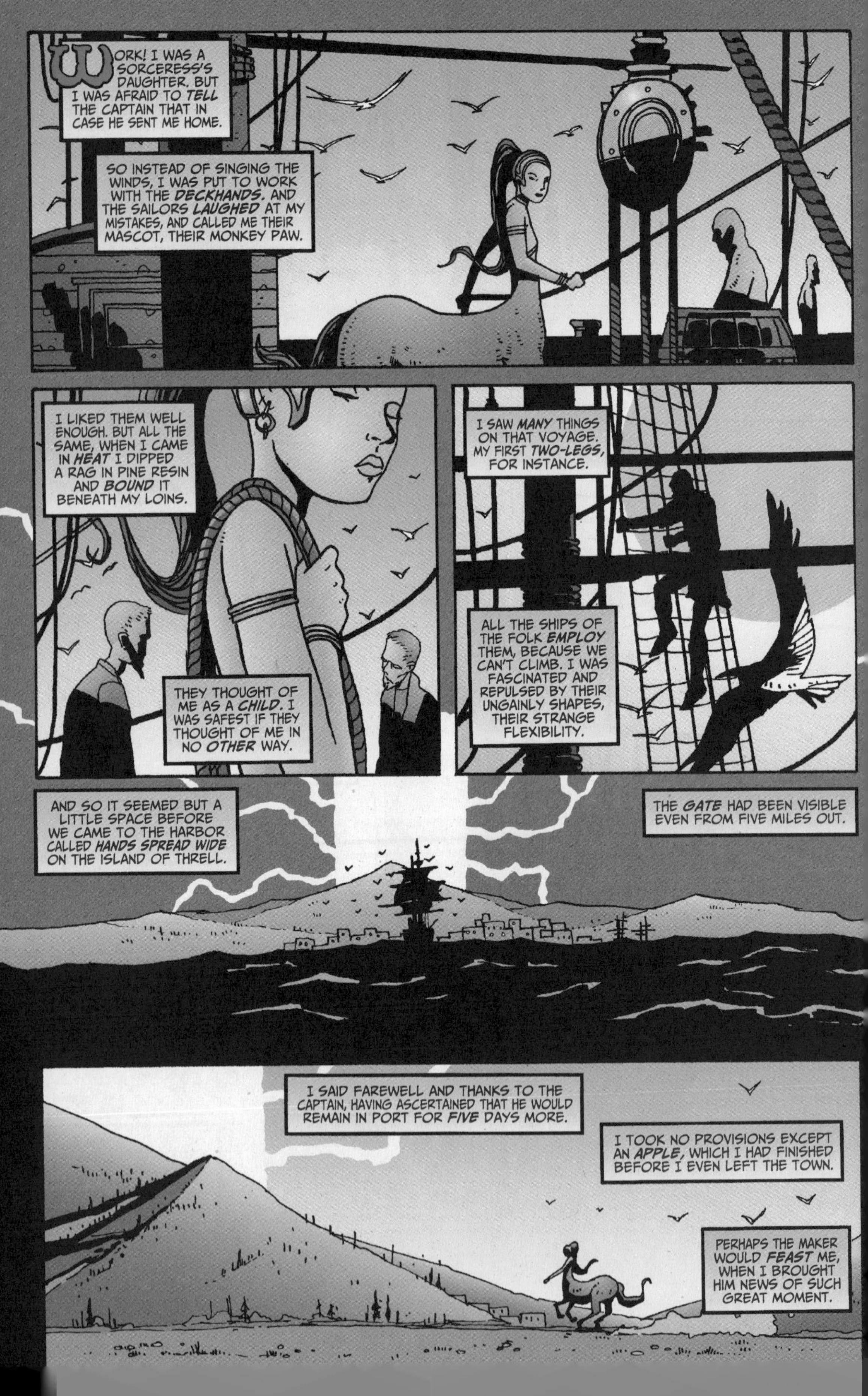
WORK! I WAS A SORCERESS'S DAUGHTER. BUT I WAS AFRAID TO TELL THE CAPTAIN THAT IN CASE HE SENT ME HOME.
SO INSTEAD OF SINGING THE WINDS, I WAS PUT TO WORK WITH THE DECKHANDS. AND THE SAILORS LAUGHED AT MY MISTAKES, AND CALLED ME THEIR MASCOT, THEIR MONKEY PAW.
I LIKED THEM WELL ENOUGH. BUT ALL THE SAME, WHEN I CAME IN HEAT I DIPPED A RAG IN PINE RESIN AND BOUND IT BENEATH MY LOINS.
THEY THOUGHT OF ME AS A CHILD. I WAS SAFEST IF THEY THOUGHT OF ME IN NO OTHER WAY.
I SAW MANY THINGS ON THAT VOYAGE. MY FIRST TWO-LEGS, FOR INSTANCE.
ALL THE SHIPS OF THE FOLK EMPLOY THEM, BECAUSE WE CAN'T CLIMB. I WAS FASCINATED AND REPULSED BY THEIR UNGAINLY SHAPES, THEIR STRANGE FLEXIBILITY.
AND SO IT SEEMED BUT A LITTLE SPACE BEFORE WE CAME TO THE HARBOR CALLED HANDS SPREAD WIDE ON THE ISLAND OF THRELL.
THE GATE HAD BEEN VISIBLE EVEN FROM FIVE MILES OUT.
I SAID FAREWELL AND THANKS TO THE CAPTAIN, HAVING ASCERTAINED THAT HE WOULD REMAIN IN PORT FOR FIVE DAYS MORE.
I TOOK NO PROVISIONS EXCEPT AN APPLE, WHICH I HAD FINISHED BEFORE I EVEN LEFT THE TOWN.
PERHAPS THE MAKER WOULD FEAST ME, WHEN I BROUGHT HIM NEWS OF SUCH GREAT MOMENT.

It was indeed a palace. Vast. And white.
And *empty.*
Maker?

Maker, I've come from Bright Holt with a warning!
I dreamed about your *death!*

The silence *fell* again, like a dusty curtain.
I'd have to leave some sort of *message* for him.
And for that I'd need either *tools* or *pigment.*

The walls were *protected* by strong wards. But they looked outwards, preventing intrusion from the world that must exist *beyond.*

But there was nothing to stop me passing through the *other* way.

KING PAK
I HAD EXPECTED A CITY OF THE GODS.
WHAT I FOUND WAS MORE LIKE SOME TWISTED DREAM.
BEER

10
APP
$1.4

BIFF
PARP PARP
PARRRRRP

OR LIKE THE LAND OF THE DEAD, IN THE STORY OF IRON-FOOTED JAEL.
A PLACE LIKE ENOUGH TO THE LIVING WORLD SO THAT EVERY REMINDER HURT ALL THE MORE.

SHE WENT IN THERE! JESUS, STU, GO AND GET A FUCKING NET OR SOMETHING!
THAT'S A DEAD END, MAN. SHE'S NOT GOING ANYWHERE.

WONDER WHAT SOMETHIN' LIKE THAT'D BE WORTH, ANYWAY.
I KNOW PEOPLE WHO'D PAY A GRAND FOR TWENTY MINUTES, KNOW WHAT I'M SAYING?
I WAS AFRAID.

TO WEAVE SPELLS REQUIRES CALM -- BUT MY MIND WAS A TUMBLING RUCK OF FEAR.
COME ON, BABY. SNIFF MY HAND. I'M A FRIEND, OKAY?
MARK, GET ROUND BEHIND HER. JUMP HER IF SHE BOLTS.
THE FOLK ARE GENTLE AND CIVILIZED. BUT SOMEWHERE IN OUR PAST THERE ARE WILD HORSES.
THE HIVES
REST IN PEACE CURTIS MAYFIELD
UHFFFF!
INSTINCT SAVED ME.

AAAAH! FUCK!
THE TWO-LEGS WERE EVERYWHERE. LIKE WORMS WHEN YOU TURN A STONE.
THE AIR WAS FULL OF ROAR AND STINK. THE NIGHT CONDENSED INTO FACES, ANGRY AND TERRIFIED.
I HAD KILLED ONE OF THEIR NUMBER AND NOW THEY WOULD HUNT ME DOWN.
BUT EVEN IN MY PANIC, CHANCE SMILED ON ME.
PAINT
WAREHOUSE
2FOR1
THE THING THAT I SOUGHT LOOMED OUT OF THE SCREAMING NIGHT AND OFFERED ITSELF TO ME.
I TOOK IT AND FLED.
TO THE MAKER'S HOUSE.
XXX
TO THE ROCK.
I HAD LEFT THE DOOR OPEN BEHIND ME -- TRUSTING IN MY INNOCENCE THAT NO ONE WOULD FIND IT.
I HAD JUST ENOUGH BREATH LEFT AS I REACHED IT TO GASP OUT THE WORD OF CLOSING.

I HAD NO BRUSH OR STYLUS.
I USED THE TOOLS THAT THE MAKER HIMSELF HAD GIVEN ME.
THE IMPORTANT THING WAS TO BE CLEAR.
TO TELL HIM OF THE DANGER IN A WAY HE COULD NOT MISTAKE OR IGNORE.
THERE WERE NO WINDOWS IN THAT PLACE. NO SUN OR STARS TO MEASURE BY. BUT I WOULD GUESS IT TOOK ME HALF A NIGHT.
I MIGHT HAVE STAYED, AND EXPLORED, AND SEEN MANY WONDERS, HAD I NOT BEEN SO HUNGRY FOR HOME.
BUT, OH --
I DID NOT EVEN KNOW WHAT HUNGER WAS.

EXCUSE ME, SIR. COULD YOU TELL ME WHERE THE SWEET WIND IS BERTHED?
IS THAT A SHIP? I NEVER 'EARD OF 'ER, GIRLIE.
NOTHIN' IN HARBOR TODAY EXCEPT THE ARROWHEAD.

I WAS HURT THAT THE CAPTAIN HAD SET SAIL WITHOUT ME. AND UNCERTAIN OF MY WELCOME ON A TWO-LEG VESSEL.
BUT THE ARROWHEAD'S SKIPPER TOOK ME ON READILY ENOUGH WHEN I TOLD HIM I WAS A SORCERESS.
MY JOURNEY HOME WAS ALL EASE AND COMFORT. I SANG THE WINDS, AND DID NOT NEED TO TROUBLE MYSELF WITH ROPES AND PINS AND CLEATS.
I THOUGHT OF MY FAMILY, AND I PROMISED MYSELF THAT I WOULD NEVER LEAVE HOME AGAIN. I HAD HAD MY FILL OF ADVENTURES.

WHEN WE CAME TO PORT I LEFT AT ONCE FOR BRIGHT HOLT. I TRAVELED THROUGH THE NIGHT AND MET NO ONE.

TEN WEEKS AFTER I HAD SET OUT I CRESTED TENWAKE HILL AND SAW THE FARMHOUSE BELOW ME, WITH BRIGHT HOLT SILENT BEYOND AND EVEN THE BIRDS STILL ASLEEP.
I WAS HOME.

FATHER! FATHER, IT'S ME!
KIRA!

OH! I... I'M SORRY. DID MY MOTHER SAY YOU COULD DRAW WATER FROM OUR WELL?
WHAT AILS YOU, CHILD? THIS FARM BELONGS TO MASTER TURJON OF IBLIS.
ARE YOU MAZED?

MASTER WHO? WHAT'S HAPPENED TO ESA-HANE, THE SORCERESS?
WHERE IS MY FAMILY?

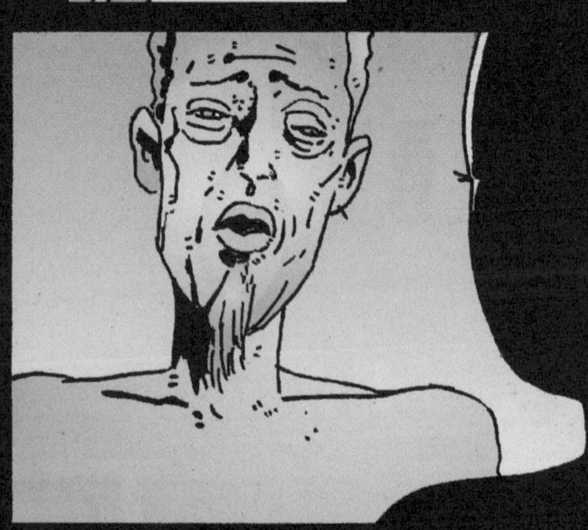

KI! KIRA! BY THE MAKER, IT'S YOU!
OW! LET GO OF ME OR I'LL TELL MY--

LOOK AT ME, KI!
DON'T GAWP LIKE A FISH! LOOK AT ME!

VALE?
OH, SWEET FATES!

WHAT HAPPENED TO YOU?
ONLY TIME, KI. TIME HAPPENS TO EVERYONE-- EXCEPT YOU, IT SEEMS.
COME, DON'T CRY. DON'T--

I HAD BEEN GONE FOR SIXTY YEARS.
AND MY MOTHER HAD DIED ONLY TEN YEARS AFTER I LEFT. DIED CALLING MY NAME, WITH THE DOCTOR STANDING HELPLESS BECAUSE SHE WASN'T EVEN SICK.
WE THOUGHT YOU WERE DEAD.
OH, KI, WE THOUGHT YOU WERE DEAD AND BURIED.

MY FATHER THREW HIMSELF ON HER FUNERAL PYRE, AS A GOOD HUSBAND SHOULD.

THEN THE TWO-LEGS CAME BACK FROM IBLIS AND TOOK THE VILLAGE. THERE WAS NO LONGER A SORCERESS TO STOP THEM.
THE BOY, ENU, WHO HAD ALMOST BEEN MY SWEETHEART, HAD DIED IN THAT BATTLE. HENCHA WAS SOLD INTO SLAVERY TO THE SEVEN CLOUDS CLAN.
AND VALE LIVED ON AS A LABORER ON THE FARM OUR FAMILY HAD OWNED FOR THREE HUNDRED YEARS.

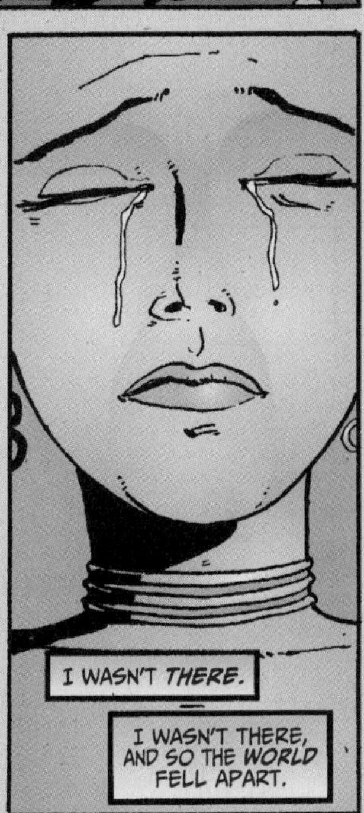
I WASN'T THERE.
I WASN'T THERE, AND SO THE WORLD FELL APART.

I WALKED AMONG THE TWO-LEGS AND THEIR HOUSES BURNED.
THOSE WHO TRIED TO RUN FROM ME BURNED ALSO.
THOSE WHO STOOD AND WAITED WENT LIKE CORN BEFORE A SCYTHE, DEAD EVEN AS THEY FELL.

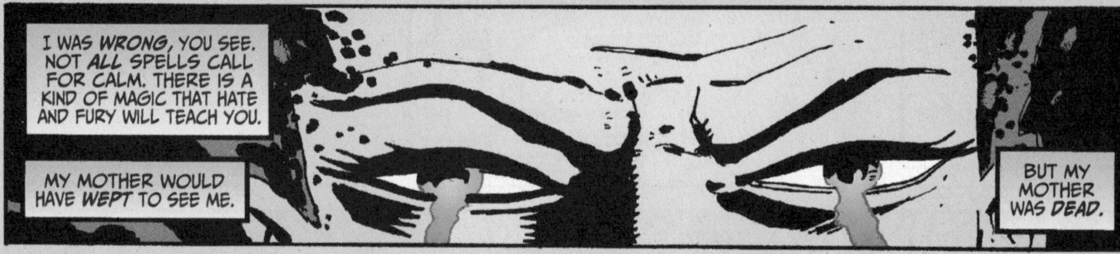
I WAS WRONG, YOU SEE. NOT ALL SPELLS CALL FOR CALM. THERE IS A KIND OF MAGIC THAT HATE AND FURY WILL TEACH YOU.
MY MOTHER WOULD HAVE WEPT TO SEE ME.
BUT MY MOTHER WAS DEAD.

THE FOLK WOULD NOT REBUILD ON EARTH THAT HAD DRUNK SO MUCH BLOOD.
BRIGHT HOLT WAS NO MORE. BUT THOSE WHO HAD SURVIVED THE TWO-LEGS' OCCUPATION BUILT A NEW VILLAGE CLOSER TO THE RIVER.
I STAYED ON AS ITS SORCERESS.

AND ANOTHER SIXTY YEARS PASSED. JUST LIKE BEFORE.
EXCEPT THAT THIS TIME I WAS THERE TO SEE THEM. AND SO THIS TIME--

--THEY MADE ME OLD.

THE PEOPLE OF RIVER HOLT GAVE ME ALL THAT IS NECESSARY FOR LIFE. EXCEPTING ONLY THEIR LOVE.
THEY HAD SEEN ME IN MY RAGE, AND AS I SAID THE FOLK ARE GENTLE AND CIVILIZED.
VALE DIED OF PLEURISY IN THE FIRST WINTER AFTER MY HOMECOMING. DIED WITHOUT ISSUE.
BUT I HAD FOUND A CHILD IN VIRKA SUTA WHO HAD THE SPARK, AND I GAVE HER THE LESSONS MY MOTHER GAVE ME.
IN THE SPRING OF MY SEVENTY-FOURTH YEAR, AS SOON AS THE FIRST EARTH WAS TURNED, I LEFT RIVER HOLT.
WITHOUT WEEPING. WITHOUT LOOKING BACK.
EVERY CAPTAIN IN GEYENISH HAD HEARD OF THE GREAT SORCERESS WHO ROUTED THE TWO-LEGS AND MADE THE SKY WEEP FIRE.
I HAD NO TROUBLE FINDING A SHIP.
THE STORY OF MY LIFE WAS COMPLETE, BUT IT WAS A STORY THAT I DID NOT UNDERSTAND.
I WANTED TO SEE THE MAKER JUST ONCE BEFORE I DIED.
I WANTED TO KNOW IF MY WARNING HAD SAVED HIM.

NOTHING HAD CHANGED.
THE AIR WAS *HEAVY* WITH THE SMELL OF THE PAINT.
THE SILENCE *HOVERED* LIKE AN ANXIOUS PARENT.

THERE WAS MY MESSAGE, AS I HAD *LEFT* IT SIXTY YEARS BEFORE.
THE WORK OF A *CHILD*. BLUNT. CRUDE--

--STILL *WET*.

I HELD *ETERNITY* IN MY HAND.
AND I SAW, IN THAT MOMENT, HOW *SMALL* A THING MY LIFE WAS IN THE MAKER'S SCALES.
HOW CENTAURS AND MEN MUST SEEM LIKE *MAYFLIES* TO HIM, THAT DANCE FOR A DAY AND THEN ARE GONE.

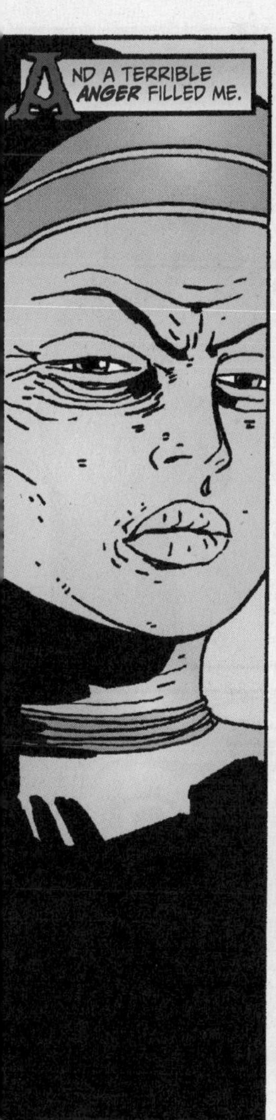

AND A TERRIBLE ANGER FILLED ME.

MY WHOLE LIFE.
EVERYTHING I HAD DONE, AND LEFT UNDONE.

I DROWNED IT IN LURID PIGMENT AND SMEARED IT OUT.
AND I CURSED IT AND DROWNED IT SOME MORE.

I'M CERTAIN I DIDN'T ASK FOR THIS TO BE DONE.

TO BE HONEST, I FIND THE COLORS A TOUCH SUBDUED.

THERE WAS NO DOUBT IN MY MIND THAT THIS WAS THE MAKER. I HAD SEEN HIM SO OFTEN IN MY DREAMS.
MY FORELEGS BUCKLED AND I GROVELED INVOLUNTARILY, ALL STRENGTH DRAINING OUT OF ME.

YOU'RE FROM MY WORLD.
YES, MAKER. I AM.
THEN WHAT ARE YOU DOING HERE?

I CAME TO BRING YOU A MESSAGE.
BUT THEN I CHANGED MY MIND.

A MESSAGE. I SEE.
WELL, IF THAT WAS WHAT YOU WERE UP TO, I'LL OVERLOOK THE INTRUSION.

BUT DON'T PUSH IT.
YOU'RE UNLIKELY TO FIND ME IN SUCH A MELLOW MOOD TWICE RUNNING.

I STOOD AND CROSSED TO THE GATE.
MY LEGS SHAKING. MY BACK *BURNING* FROM THE TOUCH OF HIS GAZE.

BUT ON THE THRESHOLD I STOPPED.
IT WAS SOMETHING I SAW IN A *DREAM.*

A WARNING.
REALLY?
OF A DANGER TO YOU.

BUT THEN YOU CHANGED YOUR *MIND* AS YOU SAID.
I SUPPOSE I'LL HAVE TO DO WITHOUT IT.

THIS TIME I CAME BACK IN DEEP WINTER.
THAT STRUCK ME AS *FITTING* SOMEHOW, FOR ALL THINGS SEEMED TO BE ENDING.
AND THE TREMBLE IN MY STEP HAD *NOTHING* TO DO WITH THE COLD.

THE STRAIT WAS FROZEN. NO SHIPS WOULD COME UNTIL THE SPRING THAW.
IN THE MEANTIME I EARNED MY KEEP HEALING SPLIT HOOVES AND SINGING LURES INTO THE CRAB-FISHERS' POTS.
SOMETIMES I IMAGINED MYSELF A CHILD AGAIN, FOR THESE WERE THE FIRST SPELLS MY MOTHER EVER TAUGHT ME.
IN THE MONTH OF FOGS, THE TABOR SET SAIL FROM THRELL WITH A CARGO OF GRAIN AND SILVER, BOUND FOR SHALAKAI.
I SIGNED ON BOARD AS WINDSINGER. WITHOUT WEEPING. WITHOUT LOOKING BACK.
AND AS WE MADE OUR SLOW WAY NORTH, I CHANCED TO LOOK UP.
A CHARIOT PASSED OVERHEAD, ITS SHADOW SKITTERING LIKE A LIVING THING ACROSS THE DECK, ACROSS MY SOUL.
I KNEW IT AT ONCE FOR A DREADFUL PORTENT.
BUT I AM AN OLD WOMAN AND I AM DONE WITH PORTENTS NOW.
MY DREAMS ARE OF THE PAST.
PERHAPS THERE, AT LEAST, I WILL FIND A WELCOME.
NEXT: PURGATORIO

WHAT SEASON WAS THIS?
ICY RAIN ENFILADED THE LOWLAND PLAINS, UNTIL THE CROPS THAT NO ONE GATHERED STARED UPWARDS FROM THE BEDS OF TROUBLED LAKES.

BUT THE SNOW STILL HELD THE NORTHERN HEIGHTS, AND IT SHOWED NO SIGN OF LETTING GO.
SPRING WOULD BE LATE, IF IT CAME AT ALL.

THIS WORLD'S NEW RULERS WAITED AND WATCHED.
AND WHILE THEY WATCHED THEY MEDITATED.
ON ABSENCE.

JILL PRESTO SLEPT MOST DAYS, IN A CHAMBER WALLED WITH GOLD.
WHEN SHE WOKE SHE WEPT, EXHAUSTED HERSELF WITH GRIEF, AND FELL AGAIN TO SLUMBER.

IN HER DREAMS HER FATHER TOLD HER GREAT SECRETS. PROMISED THAT ALL WOULD BE WELL.

BUT THE ARM SHE HUGGED TO HER CHEST ENDED IN A RAW STUMP.
AND EVEN IN HER DREAMS SHE KNEW THAT HER FATHER HAD DIED AT THE END OF A ROPE.

IN VILLAGES AND TOWNS AND CITIES THE PEOPLE WAITED FOR NEWS, BUT NO NEWS CAME.

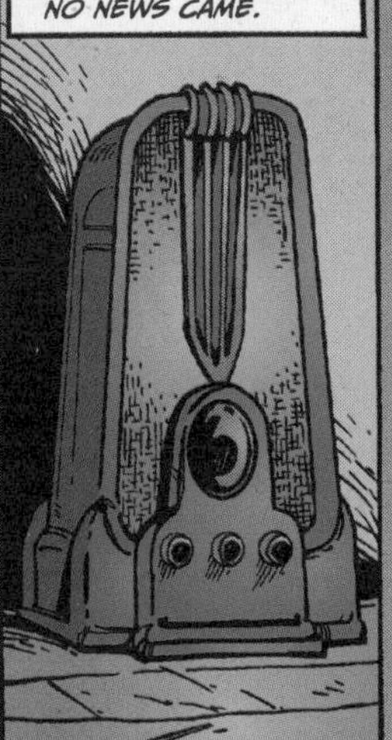

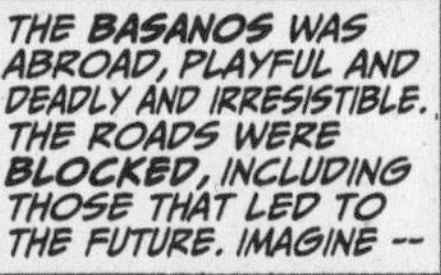
THE BASANOS WAS ABROAD, PLAYFUL AND DEADLY AND IRRESISTIBLE. THE ROADS WERE BLOCKED, INCLUDING THOSE THAT LED TO THE FUTURE. IMAGINE --

--A WHOLE WORLD LEARNING HOW TO PRAY.

IT WAS THE EIGHTH DAY.
A WEEK HAD PASSED SINCE THE MORNINGSTAR FELL BURNING OUT OF THE SKY. AN ANNUNCIATION FOR A WORLD WITH NO GODS.
THE BASANOS HAD RIDDEN IN TRIUMPH OVER THE REELING CITIES.
"BEHOLD", THEY SAID, "WE ARE COME!" AND EVERY MAN, WOMAN AND CHILD HEARD THOSE WORDS AS AN INSINUATING WHISPER CLOSE TO THEIR EAR.
AN ANNUNCIATION, HERALDING A TERRIBLE BIRTH.
THE CHILD AND THE DEATH STRETCHED OUT THEIR HANDS AS ONE, AND THE GROUND HEAVED.
PURGATORIO
MIKE CAREY WRITER PETER GROSS AND RYAN KELLY ARTISTS
DANIEL VOZZO COLORIST AND SEPARATIONS COMICRAFT LETTERING
CHRISTOPHER MOELLER COVER PAINTER MARIAH HUEHNER ASSISTANT EDITOR
SHELLY BOND EDITOR • BASED ON CHARACTERS CREATED BY GAIMAN, KIETH AND DRINGENBERG
PART 1 OF 3

ENTROPY UNDID ITSELF.
STONE CRAWLED OVER STONE, AND GROPED BLINDLY UPWARDS.
THERE WAS A HARVEST AFTER ALL.
IF YOU WANTED TO LOOK AT IT THAT WAY.

I KNOW. I KNOW IT'S BEEN DONE. BUT IT'S NOT LIKE IT'S A LONG LIST.

STEVIE WONDER. THAT PUNK GUY WHO HAD POLIO.
HARPO MARX.

I'M SORRY.
I'M JUST NOT THAT STRONG.

HHHHHHH!

IN THE INTERESTS OF SECURITY AND STABILITY, JILL PRESTO, CERTAIN BASIC FREEDOMS HAVE BEEN SUSPENDED.
I ASSURE YOU, IT'S ONLY TEMPORARY.
MAGICIAN

ALL OUR POWER IS FOCUSED ON YOU. YOU ARE A PRISM THROUGH WHICH DESTINY BENDS AS IT PASSES.
THE SUN COULD SOONER DOUSE ITSELF IN THE SEA THAN YOUR BODY COULD SUSTAIN A WOUND.
THEN WHAT'S THIS?
YOU FUCKING CARDBOARD CUT-OUT SON OF A BITCH, WHAT'S THIS?
A REMINDER. THAT WHAT WE HAVE GIVEN WE CAN TAKE AWAY.
OKAY. TAKE IT. PLEASE? I'VE HAD ENOUGH.
I DON'T WANT TO SEE ANY MORE OF THIS.
THAT'S IMPOSSIBLE. BUT WE WOULD HAVE YOU BE HAPPY WITH YOUR BARGAIN.
IF YOU RENEW YOUR OATH TO US, WE WILL RESTORE YOUR HAND.

FUCK YOU.
YOU PULLED THE CITY DOWN ON ALL THOSE PEOPLE. AND IF YOU SHOULD EVER HAPPEN TO BE DISEMBOWELED I'D CHEERFULLY USE YOUR GUTS AS FAIRY LIGHTS.
WELL, THEN THERE'S NOTHING TO BE SAID. FOR A FEW HOURS MORE, WE ARE DIVIDED.
BUT WHEN WE'RE ALL MET, WE'LL BEGIN.
BEGIN? BEGIN WHAT? YOU ALREADY CONQUERED THE FUCKING WORLD!
CONQUEST WAS A MEANS TO AN END. TO A LOYAL SERVANT I MIGHT HAVE EXPLAINED.
BUT YOU WOULD NOT BE OUR SERVANT. SO NOW YOU WILL BE OUR TOOL.
"THE DIFFERENCE IS THAT A TOOL CAN BE DISCARDED AFTER USE.
"AS YOU WILL BE."

SHOOOOOM
DEPLOY!

NO OPPOSING FORCES, WAR LEADER. AT LEAST--
I SEE HIM, LOTH.
MOUNT A *PERIMETER,* AND AWAIT MY ORDERS.
LORD LUCIFER?
I THINK NOT.
I'LL SEND OUT A HERALD.
NO.
I'LL SEE FOR MYSELF.

WHAT BUSINESS HAVE *YOUR* KIND HERE?
I BRING YOU *EXCELLENT* NEWS, DAUGHTER OF LILITH...
LUCIFER IS *DEAD*.
SLAIN BY THE BASANOS.

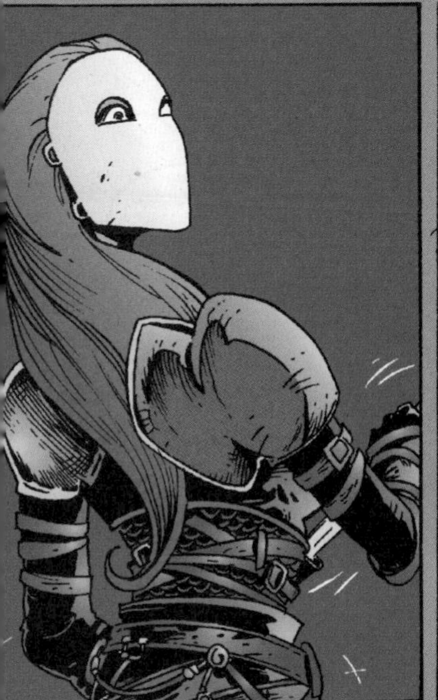

SHINNNNNG

YOUR... REACTION IS... CHIMERICAL AND... ILL-JUDGED. I PROPOSE AN *ALLIANCE*.

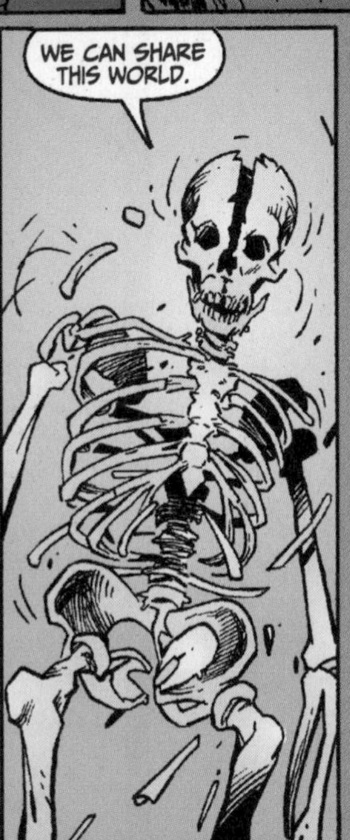

WE CAN SHARE THIS WORLD.

IT'S NOT YOURS TO DISPOSE OF. IF LUCIFER IS DEAD THEN SHOW ME THE BODY.
HE *IS* DEAD. BELIEVE ME. NOTHING THAT *LIVES* COULD HAVE SURVIVED THE BLOW WE STRUCK.

BUT AS TO THE *BODY*, I CONFESS --

"--WE'VE TEMPORARILY LOST IT."
WELL WHAT ABOUT THAT ONE?
NO, IT DOESN'T FEEL RIGHT. IT'S ANOTHER FALSE TRAIL.
WHOEVER TOOK HIM KNEW THAT THE BASANOS WOULD WANT TO MAKE SURE HE WAS DEAD...
YEAH, WELL THEY PROBABLY GOT SIMILAR FEELINGS ABOUT YOU, PRINCESS.
EVEN WITH THE BIG MAN DOWN YOU'RE A SPANNER IN THE WOODPILE, KNOW WHAT I MEAN?
DOWN THERE!
OW! SHIT! WARN ME BEFORE YOU DO THAT! DOWN THERE WHAT?
SOMETHING.
SOMETHING ALIVE.

THREE MILES UP ON A *MOUNTAIN*?!

UNDER THE MOUNTAIN.

OH, FUCKING WONDERFUL!

LOOK, I'VE GOT A *BODY*, REMEMBER? I MEAN, RIGHT HERE. THIS IS ME.

I CAN'T *DO* THE "NOW I'M SOLID, NOW I'M NOT" ROUTINE!

THEN WAIT HERE. I'M GOING IN.
OH SURE, I'LL *SUNBATHE*! WHATTA YOU MEAN, WAIT?
HOW LONG FOR?
UNTIL I COME BACK.

I LET PEOPLE TAKE *ADVANTAGE* OF ME.
THAT'S ALWAYS BEEN MY PROBLEM.

THE DANCE WILL CALL FOR SUPREME CONCENTRATION AND EFFORT.
YOU SHOULD NOT BE DOING THIS.
I DISAGREE.
WE'VE SPENT MUCH OF OUR CONSCIOUS EXISTENCE IN A BOX OF OAK AND IRON.
AT THIS MOMENT, OF ALL MOMENTS, I'LL NOT HAVE THE VAULT OF THE SKY REMINDING ME OF THAT PRISON.
WE HAVE SEARCHED THE ENTIRE MOUNTAIN RANGE FROM END TO END. THE BODY ISN'T THERE.
THEN WHAT? SAY HE'S ALIVE, AFTER ALL.
BLIND. BURNED. CONSUMED AND CORED BY HIS OWN FIERCE HEAT.
TO EVERY THING THERE IS A SEASON. TONIGHT WE DANCE.
TOMORROW IS TIME ENOUGH TO SCATTER LORD LUCIFER'S ASHES.

THEY SAID WHAT?
THAT THEY WOULD SHARE THIS WORLD WITH US -- SPLIT IT INTO TWO EQUAL-SIZED PARTS.
IT MAKES NO SENSE.
WHAT STRATEGY WOULD LEAD THEM TO GIVE AWAY WHAT THEY'VE FOUGHT SO HARD TO WIN?
THEY DON'T INTEND TO GIVE IT AWAY.
THEY WANT A RESPITE, THAT'S ALL. AND IF PROMISES WILL BUY IT FOR THEM, THEY'LL DISPENSE PROMISES LIKE WATER.
SO WHAT ARE WE TO DO? ATTACK?
WE KNOW NOTHING ABOUT THEM EXCEPT THAT THEY SAY THEY DEFEATED AND KILLED THE MORNINGSTAR.
WHAT WILL WE DO? WE WILL ACCEPT.
AND THEN WE'LL FIND OUT MORE.

ELAINE LET THE SOLID FORM SHE HAD IMAGINED FOR HERSELF DISSOLVE BACK INTO AIRY SPIRIT. HER REAL BODY WAS STILL LYING BENEATH THE RUBBLE IN THE LONDON UNDERGROUND.
SHE SLID DOWN THROUGH THE ROCK LIKE LIGHT THROUGH LACE.
SHE WAS HOMING IN ON THE SINGLE SPARK OF LIFE AND WARMTH IN ALL THAT WILDERNESS OF ICE.
SHE WAS HOPING THAT IT WAS LUCIFER.
BUT EVEN FROM WHERE I WAS SITTING, LUCIFER'S SPARK WAS TOO FAINT TO FIND.
NO.
IT WAS ME SHE SENSED.
COME CLOSER, GIRL.
YOU WON'T SEE MUCH FROM BACK THERE.
YOU CAN SEE ME!
MORE CLEARLY THAN THIS CAVE, OR THESE MOUNTAINS.
TO MANY EYES, YOU ARE SUPERLATIVELY VISIBLE.

OH MY GOD! IS THAT--?
LORD LUCIFER. I'M AFRAID SO.
IT LOOKS... VERY BAD.
IT'S *WORSE* THAN IT LOOKS. THE EXTERNAL COMBUSTION IS A SIGN OF EVEN MORE APPALLING DAMAGE *ELSEWHERE.*
WILL HE DIE?
I DON'T THINK I COULD *BEAR* IT IF HE DIED.
HE IS MADE OF *WILL,* AS YOUR FATHER MICHAEL IS MADE OF POWER. HE MIGHT SURVIVE IN SPITE OF EVERYTHING.
I HAVE BEEN DOING WHAT LITTLE I COULD TO *MEND* HIM.
BECAUSE IF HE DIES, SOMETHING *TERRIBLE* IS GOING TO HAPPEN.
AND IT WILL ALL BE MY FAULT.

"YOU SEE, THEY ARE NOT CARDS. NOT TRULY. ANY MORE THAN YOU ARE FLESH, TRULY.
"IT WAS AN ARBITRARY DECISION AT THE DESIGN STAGE.
"AS THEY TOOK SHAPE UNDER MY HANDS, I CAUGHT A GLIMPSE OF THE PARADOX THAT I WAS CREATING.
"READERS AND RECORDERS OF DESTINY, BUT WITH A LIVING THING'S FREEDOM TO DECIDE AND ACT.
"IF REALITY IS A MAGIC LANTERN SHOW, THEY ARE THE LENSES THROUGH WHICH ALL THE INFINITE POSSIBILITIES OF SHAPE AND COLOR ARE FOCUSED.
"IT WAS NECESSARY TO HOBBLE THEM IN SOME WAY. OR WE WOULD ALL BECOME THEIR SERVANTS.
"AND IT WAS HERE THAT THEIR DESIGN WAS A HELP TO ME.
WHAT DO YOU MEAN?
IT SEEMED... EASY, AND SENSIBLE, TO DENY THEM SOME OF THE OTHER PREROGATIVES OF LIVING THINGS.
TO MAKE THEM FINITE, IN THAT RESPECT AT LEAST.

BUT MY ***CONTROL*** OVER THEM WAS AN ILLUSION.

YOU'RE FREE NOW!

WHERE IS THE ***POINT*** IN WEARING CHAINS?

OH YES, IN OUR ***OWN*** CREATION THERE WERE THINGS THEY COULDN'T DO. ***PROHIBITIONS*** I'D LAID DOWN.

"SO THEY JUST CAME ***HERE*** INSTEAD."

SORRY. I STILL DON'T UNDERSTAND.
I'M NOT EXPLAINING IT VERY WELL. PERHAPS AN *EXAMPLE* WOULD BE BETTER.
LOOK.
YOU'RE AN *ANGEL.* LIKE ME.
I'M MELEOS OF THE SERAPHIM, AND I'M NOT LIKE YOU AT ALL. *NOBODY* IS LIKE YOU.
YOU'RE *MICHAEL'S* DAUGHTER. WHICH IS ACTUALLY MY *POINT.*
YOU SEE, MICHAEL IS *STERILE.*
FOR HIM TO *HAVE* A DAUGHTER, THE RULES HAD TO BE BROKEN.
OH! YOU MEAN THEY'RE GOING TO... UMM...
NOT GOING TO.
THEY'RE DOING IT *NOW.*

"AND IN THE NEXT GENERATION, I IMAGINE THEY'LL BREED FOR STRENGTH."

SHE RAN, THEN.
WITHOUT LOOKING BACK.
THE WRITHING THING IN THE SKY HAD REACHED ITS CLIMAX.
HOW SHE COULD HAVE KNOWN WHAT THAT MEANT FOR HER, I CANNOT GUESS.
BUT SHE KNEW. AND SO SHE RAN.
DOWN CORRIDORS OF COLD STONE THAT SOMEHOW HAD THE ORGANIC INTIMACY OF A WASPS' NEST.
AND THE LIGHT GROWING STRONGER AT HER BACK REPORTED ON HER PROGRESS IN SARDONIC STROBE.

THEY CAUGHT HER AS SHE FELL.
TRANSFIXED HER A MILLION TIMES IN THE SPACE OF A SECOND.

AND WHEN SHE TRIED TO SCREAM, THE RUSHING AIR PLUCKED THE BREATH OUT OF HER MOUTH.

BUT THEY STOPPED HER A LONG TIME BEFORE SHE HIT THE GROUND, OF COURSE. SHE WAS TOO PRECIOUS NOW TO UNDERGO SUCH SHOCK.
A HUMAN BEING REGRESSED TO THE FIRST FORGOTTEN MOMENT OF HER OWN HISTORY.

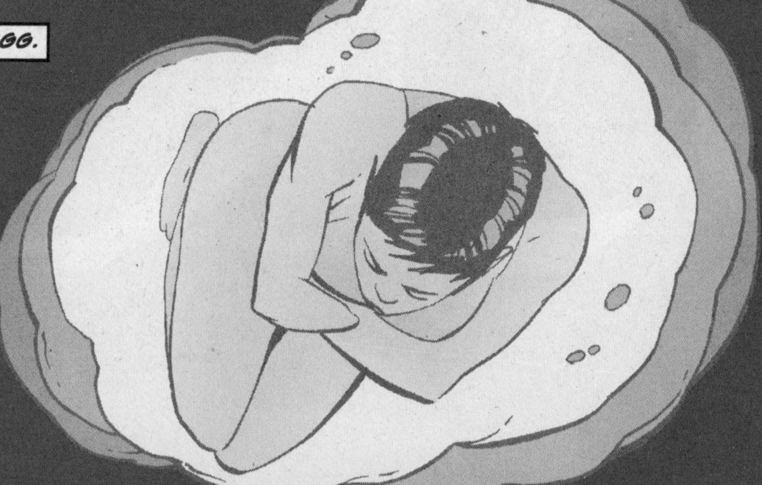
A FERTILIZED EGG.

FROM BIRTH TO DEATH. HOW SMALL OUR CIRCUITS ARE.
HOW UNERRINGLY WE FIND THE PATHS THAT WILL UNMAKE US.
EVEN WE WHO CALL OURSELVES IMMORTAL.
HMM.
THAT BAD, EH?
I KNOW, I KNOW. NOT QUITE TIME, YET.
BUT THIS ONE I HAD TO SEE FOR MYSELF.
TO BE CONTINUED

"IT'S HARD.

HARD TO GET THE DISTANCE RIGHT.
I CAN'T--

"OH."

"OKAY, NOW I'M--
"I'M SOMEWHERE CLOSE.

SOMEWHERE VERY CLOSE.

WHAT DO YOU SEE?

"THREE MEN--

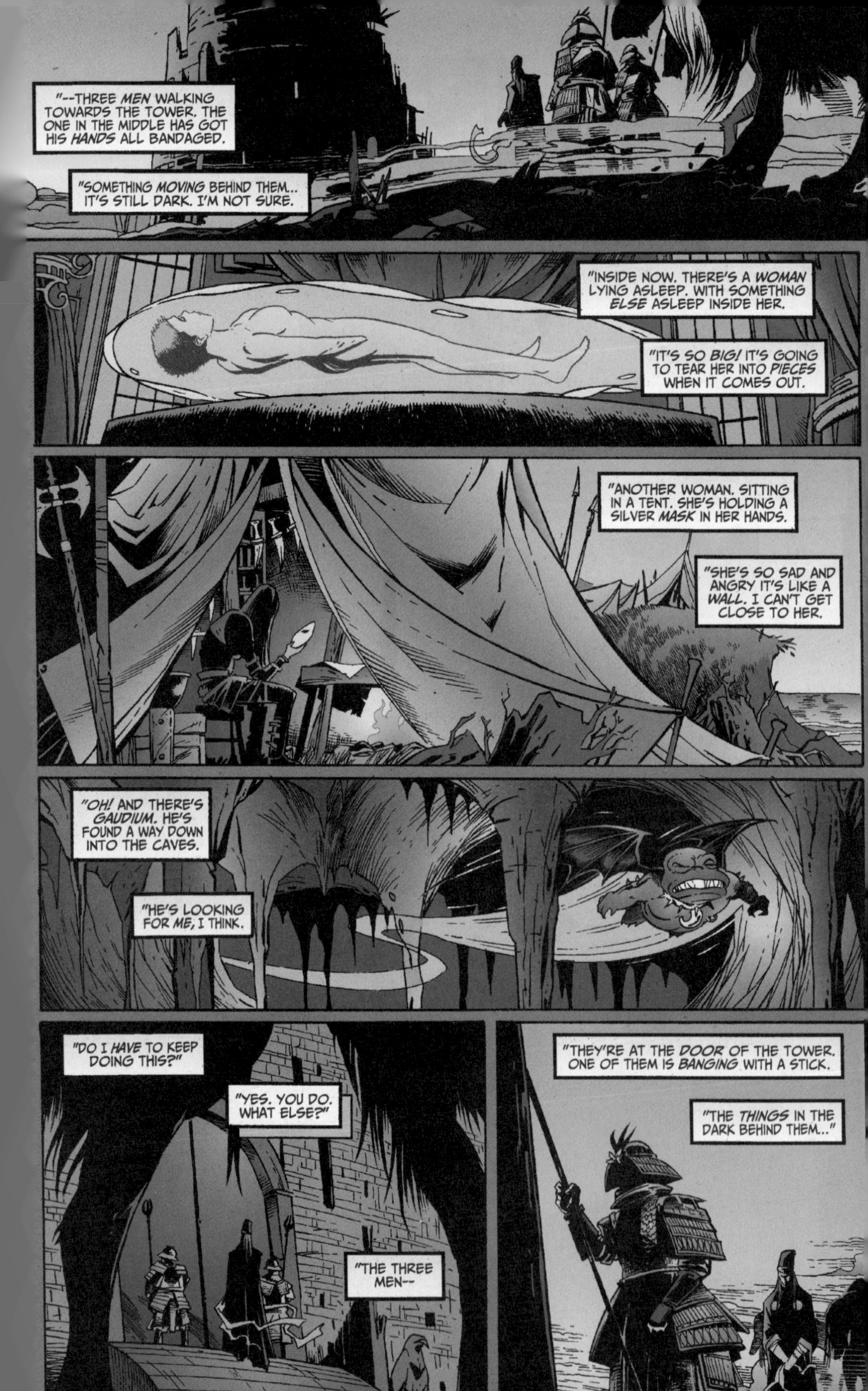
"--THREE MEN WALKING TOWARDS THE TOWER. THE ONE IN THE MIDDLE HAS GOT HIS HANDS ALL BANDAGED.
"SOMETHING MOVING BEHIND THEM.. IT'S STILL DARK. I'M NOT SURE.
"INSIDE NOW. THERE'S A WOMAN LYING ASLEEP. WITH SOMETHING ELSE ASLEEP INSIDE HER.
"IT'S SO BIG! IT'S GOING TO TEAR HER INTO PIECES WHEN IT COMES OUT.
"ANOTHER WOMAN. SITTING IN A TENT. SHE'S HOLDING A SILVER MASK IN HER HANDS.
"SHE'S SO SAD AND ANGRY IT'S LIKE A WALL. I CAN'T GET CLOSE TO HER.
"OH! AND THERE'S GAUDIUM. HE'S FOUND A WAY DOWN INTO THE CAVES.
"HE'S LOOKING FOR ME, I THINK.
"DO I HAVE TO KEEP DOING THIS?"
"YES. YOU DO. WHAT ELSE?"
"THE THREE MEN--
"THEY'RE AT THE DOOR OF THE TOWER. ONE OF THEM IS BANGING WITH A STICK.
"THE THINGS IN THE DARK BEHIND THEM..."

I CAN SEE WHAT THEY ARE NOW.
"THEY'RE DOGS!
"THEY'RE GREAT BIG DOGS!
PURGATORIO
MIKE CAREY WRITER PETER GROSS AND RYAN KELLY ARTISTS
COMICRAFT LETTERING DANIEL VOZZO COLORS AND SEPARATIONS
CHRISTOPHER MOELLER COVER PAINTER MARIAH HUEHNER ASSISTANT EDITOR
SHELLY BOND EDITOR • BASED ON CHARACTERS CREATED BY GAIMAN, KIETH AND DRINGENBERG
PART 2 OF 3

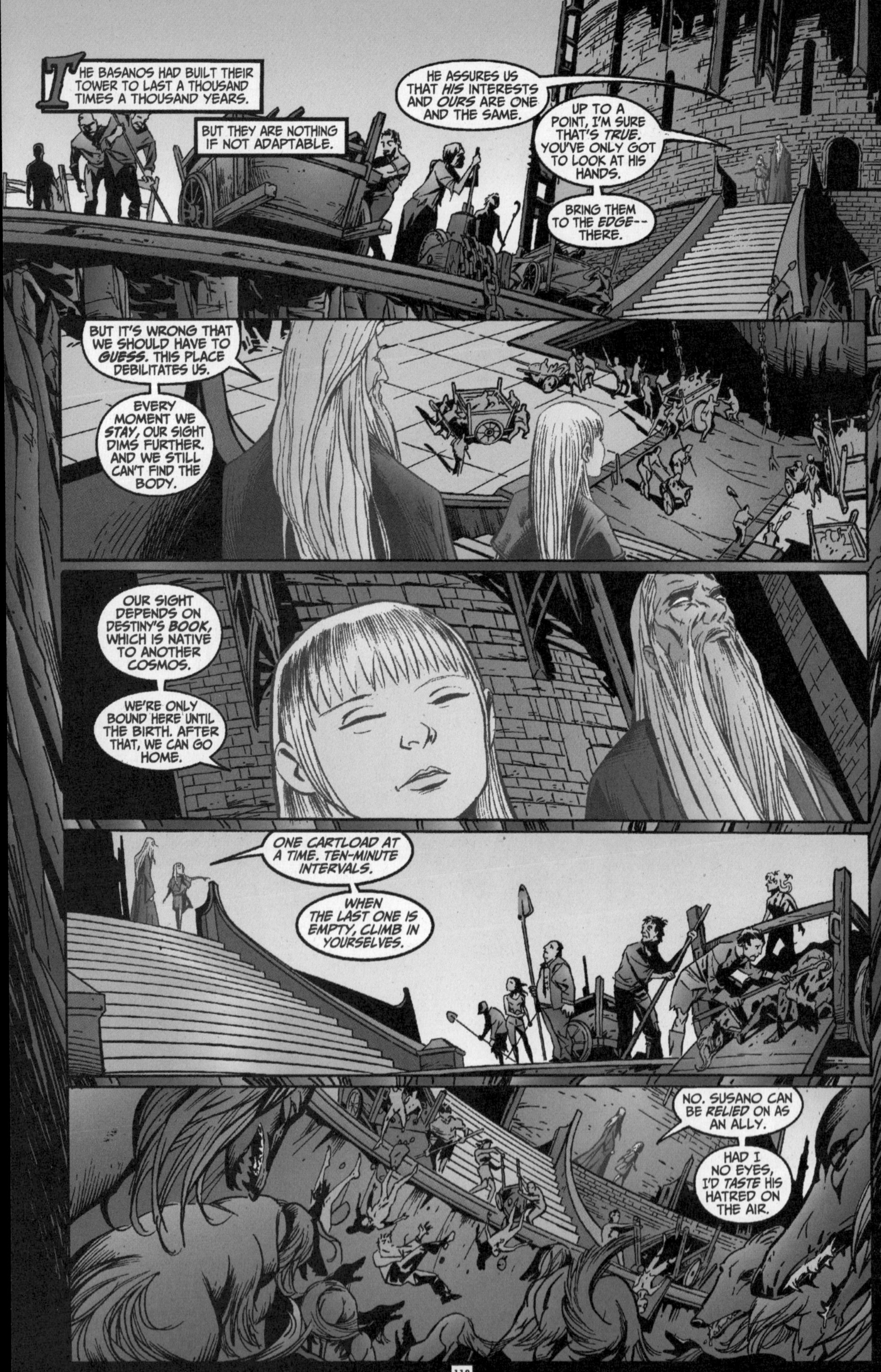
THE BASANOS HAD BUILT THEIR TOWER TO LAST A THOUSAND TIMES A THOUSAND YEARS.
BUT THEY ARE NOTHING IF NOT ADAPTABLE.
HE ASSURES US THAT HIS INTERESTS AND OURS ARE ONE AND THE SAME.
UP TO A POINT, I'M SURE THAT'S TRUE. YOU'VE ONLY GOT TO LOOK AT HIS HANDS.
BRING THEM TO THE EDGE-- THERE.
BUT IT'S WRONG THAT WE SHOULD HAVE TO GUESS. THIS PLACE DEBILITATES US.
EVERY MOMENT WE STAY, OUR SIGHT DIMS FURTHER. AND WE STILL CAN'T FIND THE BODY.
OUR SIGHT DEPENDS ON DESTINY'S BOOK, WHICH IS NATIVE TO ANOTHER COSMOS.
WE'RE ONLY BOUND HERE UNTIL THE BIRTH. AFTER THAT, WE CAN GO HOME.
ONE CARTLOAD AT A TIME. TEN-MINUTE INTERVALS.
WHEN THE LAST ONE IS EMPTY, CLIMB IN YOURSELVES.
NO. SUSANO CAN BE RELIED ON AS AN ALLY.
HAD I NO EYES, I'D TASTE HIS HATRED ON THE AIR.

YOU SEE HOW FAR YOUR SPIRIT RANGED?
YEAH, BUT I WAS SCARED. I DIDN'T KNOW IF I COULD FIND MY WAY BACK.
BACK TO WHAT? YOUR BODY LIES BROKEN AND BLEEDING IN ANOTHER WORLD.
AND YOUR SOUL IS NO MORE ANCHORED TO THIS PLACE THAN TO ANY OF THE OTHER PLACES YOU VISITED.
BUT IT IS. I MEAN, I'M HERE, AREN'T I? THIS IS ME.
IN A SENSE, PERHAPS. BUT ONLY BECAUSE YOU'VE DECIDED THAT THIS WILL BE SO.
LISTEN TO ME, ELAINE.
WHEN GOD MADE THE WORLD, THE FIRST THING HE CREATED WAS THE HOST OF HEAVEN. BEGINNING WITH YOUR FATHER, MICHAEL--
--AND LUCIFER.
"FOR EVERYTHING ELSE THAT WAS MADE, THEY WERE HIS INTERMEDIARIES.
"MICHAEL'S DEMIURGIC POWER GAVE BIRTH TO THE FIRST MATTER.
"AND LUCIFER'S WILL SHAPED IT INTO SUNS.

YOU'RE NOT GOING TO ANSWER MY QUESTION, ARE YOU?
I AM ANSWERING IT. BUT YOU MAY NOT UNDERSTAND OR ACCEPT WHAT I TELL YOU.
SEE HERE IS A FLAME.
VOLATILE GASES, FLARING INTO INCANDESCENCE JUST BECAUSE THEY'VE BEEN HEATED UP.
WHERE THE FLAME GOES, WOOD TURNS INTO CHARCOAL, WATER INTO STEAM, FLESH INTO ASH.
BUT HE IS NOT FLESH. AND YOU ARE NOT FLESH.
AND THE FLAME HAS MOVED ON.
I'VE BEEN TRYING TO HEAL HIM. SPLICING MY OWN LIFE FORCE TO HIS.
BUT IT HASN'T WORKED. MY MAKER DIDN'T DESIGN ME AS A CONDUIT FOR POWER ON THAT SCALE.
TELL ME, ELAINE. IF YOU COULD SAVE LUCIFER BY RUNNING A SINGLE ERRAND FOR ME, WOULD YOU DO IT?
WOULD I--WOULD I SAVE...?
DON'T BE STUPID! WHERE DO YOU WANT ME TO GO?
IN THERE.

YUHHH...
YYYOU..
YOU... HAVE...
...NO CLAIM ON ME.
NEVER SAID I DID.
BUT THE BIG WHEELS ARE TURNING, OBVIOUSLY. EVERYONE NEEDS TO KNOW WHAT HAPPENS NEXT.

WHAT HAPPENS NEXT...IS THAT... I REINSTATE MYSELF.
AND THEN I DESTROY THE BASANOS.
HHHHHHHH!
OR PERHAPS--
--YOU DON'T, RIGHT.
IT'S LIKE THE END OF THAT MOVIE--THE ITALIAN JOB--WHERE THE BUS IS HALFWAY OFF THE CLIFF?
I MEAN, YOU'RE SO CLOSE TO THE EDGE THAT EVEN TRYING TO PULL YOURSELF BACK WILL SEND YOU OVER.
TOUGH CALL. REALLY.
THEN I'LL WAIT.
UNTIL ANOTHER OPTION COMES ALONG.

IT IS MY MOTHER'S WISH THAT SHE AND THE BASANOS MIGHT BE ON TERMS OF THE WARMEST AMITY.
AND SO WE ARE, NOBLE SUSANO. OUR ATTACK ON LUCIFER COULD NOT HAVE SUCCEEDED WITHOUT HER.
HOW ARE YOUR HANDS, BY THE WAY?
I THANK YOU FOR YOUR SOLICITUDE. THERE IS SOME HOPE THEY WILL HEAL.
AND YOUR VESSEL? IS SHE WELL?
AH. I APOLOGIZE PROFUSELY.
I HAVE BEEN INDISCREET.

THE VESSEL SLEEPS. SHE'LL SLEEP UNTIL SHE IS DELIVERED OF OUR CHILDREN.
BUT THAT ISN'T WHY YOU'VE COME HERE.
MY MOTHER BELIEVES THAT LORD LUCIFER LIVES.
IF HE LIVES, HE WILL RECOVER. IF HE RECOVERS, WE ARE ALL LOST BEYOND REDEMPTION.
SO I BROUGHT YOU A GIFT.
THE ANIMALS? THEIR DIET IS A LITTLE TROUBLESOME TO SUPPLY.
THEY BELONGED TO MY BROTHER, KAGUTSUCHI, WHO IS NOW DEAD.
HE DOTED ON THEM.
HUNTING WAS HIS GREATEST JOY.

IT'S BEEN A LONG, LONG TIME.
HASN'T IT? SINCE YOU STARTED THE BALL ROLLING, I MEAN.
THE BALL?
THE UNIVERSE. THE BIG BANG.
THE FIRST BIG BANG.
NOT THE ENCORE.
NONE OF THIS WAS OF MY CHOOSING.
NO?
THAT'S NOT THE WAY I SEE IT.
YOU AND MICHAEL WERE HIS FIRST BIG IDEAS. YOU CAME OUT PRETTY MUCH UNDILUTED.
"HERE," HE SAYS. "I WANT A UNIVERSE. RUN ONE UP FOR ME."

IT'S NO SURPRISE YOU TURNED OUT THE WAY YOU DID.
I GUESS HE'D HAVE GOTTEN BORED WITH FOLLOWING ORDERS, TOO.
I HAVE NOTHING IN COMMON WITH YAHWEH. AND THIS ISN'T A TOPIC I'M INTERESTED IN PURSUING.
OH, COME ON! WHEN AM I GOING TO GET ANOTHER CHANCE?
I MEAN, HERE YOU ARE. STUCK AT THE BUS STOP UNTIL THE NEXT MIRACLE ROLLS UP.
AND THESE ARE JUST THINGS I'VE BEEN DYING TO SAY.
I INTEND TO SURVIVE THIS.
ANYTHING YOU SAY OUGHT TO TAKE THAT INTO ACCOUNT.
YOU KNOW, I TOLD MY BROTHER ONCE, THAT IF YOU KILL THE MESSENGER--
--IN THE LONG RUN, YOU JUST GET LESS MAIL.

MELEOS, THERE'S NOTHING HERE. IT'S ALL DARK.
THAT'S AS I WOULD HAVE EXPECTED.
TRY TO FIND A GRADIENT IN THE DARK. IT'LL BE THICKER IN SOME DIRECTIONS THAN IN OTHERS.
OKAY, PAL. YOU'RE GONNA TELL ME WHERE SHE IS.
AND IF I WERE YOU, I'D TALK FAST. BECAUSE IN A MINUTE FLAT I'M GOING TO BE EATING YOUR VOCAL CORDS.
GAUDIUM-- IT'S ME.
JEEEEEESUS!
AND I AM RELIEVING YOU OF YOUR RESPONSIBILITIES HERE.
WHOA! HEY, JUST CUT THE SHIT, MELEOS, ALL RIGHT?
I'M TAKING MY ORDERS FROM HIGHER UP THAN YOU.
I'M SUPPOSED TO BE HER BODYGUARD! DON'T SEND ME--
A FALLEN CHERUB AS A BODYGUARD?
WELL, YOU SEEM TO HAVE INTERPRETED YOUR DUTIES SOMEWHAT LIBERALLY.
I'M SURE SHE HAS BEEN THREATENED BEFORE THIS...

"BY HEAVEN AS WELL AS HELL.
"BUT I THINK HER ENEMIES WOULD LAUGH IF THEY COULD SEE WHERE HER FRIENDS HAVE BROUGHT HER."

DID ANYTHING ELSE PASS BETWEEN THEM?
PROTESTATIONS THAT FELL SHORT OF PROMISES.
AND A PACK OF DOGS, THAT SUSANO BROUGHT WITH HIM FROM THE REALMS OF PAIN.
YOU'VE DONE WELL, ELOKIM SHAER. I THANK YOU.
ONLY MY DUTY, WAR LEADER.
GENTLEMEN, YOUR OPINIONS, PLEASE.
THE BASANOS ARE FORGING A COALITION. IF WE FIND OURSELVES OUTSIDE IT--
--THEN WE'LL BE THE NEXT TO FALL. MY THINKING, TOO.
BUT IF LUCIFER IS DEAD, THEN WHAT'S THE PURPOSE OF THIS HUNT?
MAZIKEEN.
WHAT DO YOU THINK?
THAT WE HAVE THE NARROWEST OF WINDOWS, AND WITHIN IT THE MOST ENORMOUS LEVERAGE.
AFTER THAT--NOTHING. UNLESS WE GUESS RIGHT.
I HAVE A PLAN.
HEAR ME OUT BEFORE YOU SPEAK.

THE CHILD'S SPIRIT TOILED ON THROUGH THE GREAT EMPTINESS. THE UNTENANTED *HOUSE* THAT WAS LUCIFER'S BODY AND BEING.

BUT SHE DID NOT *NOTICE* THE EMPTINESS. SHE DID NOT FEEL THE COLD.

THE CHOICE I HAD GIVEN HER WAS *ILLUSARY*, OF COURSE. HOW COULD SHE REFUSE?

TO BE HIS *SAVIOR*. TO BRING HIM *LIFE* IN THE BRIMMING CHALICE OF HER OWN HEART...
ONCE I HAD RAISED THAT IMAGE IN HER MIND, SHE WOULD HAVE BEGGED TO GO.

LUCIFER!
THE NEXT MIRACLE.
ANOTHER *OPTION*. IRONICALLY, ONE THAT THE *BASANOS* ALERTED ME TO.

I WAS SENT TO FIND YOU! YOU HAVE TO TAKE MY *HAND*, AND THEN I'LL BE A CONDUCTOR OR SOMETHING.
IT WILL GIVE YOU THE *STRENGTH* TO--

HI, ELAINE.
DON'T MIND ME.

UH...SO IF YOU TOUCH MY HAND, THE POWER WILL FLOW. AND YOU'LL BE ABLE TO HEAL ALL YOUR BURNS.
AND WHO TOLD YOU ALL THIS?
AN ANGEL. I DON'T REMEMBER HIS NAME.

AN ANGEL?
WELL, IT PROBABLY ALL MAKES SENSE ON SOME LEVEL. AND IT'S NOT AS THOUGH I'VE GOT ANYTHING TO LOSE.

OPEN THE WAY FOR ME, ELAINE BELLOC.

RISE SLOWLY, MORNINGSTAR, AND BE AT PEACE.
THIS PLACE IS A SECRET UNPENETRATED BY THE BASANOS AND THEIR SERVANTS.
MELEOS. HAH! NOT THE FACE I WAS EXPECTING, I ADMIT.
AFTER HAMBURG, I THOUGHT YOU'D TRY FOR SOME KIND OF REVENGE.
OH, BUT I DID.

I CONSIDERED MORE DRAMATIC GESTURES. BUT I NEEDED YOU ALIVE.
AND THIS IS REVENGE ENOUGH.
RESTORING ME TO HEALTH?
PUNCTURING THAT COCOON OF SELF-SUFFICIENCY.
MAKING YOUR LIFE CONTINGENT ON MINE.
YOU'LL ALWAYS KNOW, LUCIFER. AS LONG AS YOU EXIST, YOU'LL REMEMBER THAT YOUR LIFE WAS ONCE A GIFT IN MY BESTOWING.
YES, VERY NEAT. TELLINGLY IRONIC.
MELEOS--IN MY WINGS, THERE SHOULD HAVE BEEN TWO FEATHERS UNTOUCHED BY THE FLAME.
DID YOU FIND THEM?

YOUR FEATHERS FELL LIKE RAIN, MORNINGSTAR.
BUT THESE TWO WERE NOT MINE. THEY WERE IZANAMI'S.
AND THEY ABSORBED MOST OF MY POWER AND ESSENCE WHEN I BURNED.
BUT...BUT YOU'RE RECOVERED. YOU DON'T NEED THE FEATHERS.
WE'LL DISCUSS IT LATER.
FORGIVE ME, BUT I'D PREFER AN ANSWER NOW.
IF YOU INSIST. THE FEATHERS WILL BE EITHER CRUCIAL OR ENTIRELY TRIVIAL.
DEPENDING ON WHETHER I LIVE LONG ENOUGH TO TOUCH THEM.

YOU'RE DEATH, AREN'T YOU?
YEAH. AND YOU'RE YAHWEH'S GRAND-DAUGHTER.
I HAVEN'T SEEN YOU SINCE THAT NIGHT IN LONDON. WHEN I WAS LOOKING FOR YOUR FRIEND.
MONA DOYLE. AND YOU DIDN'T GET HER, DID YOU?
NOT RIGHT THEN. DON'T REMEMBER THE LAST TIME SOMEONE LED ME ON A DANCE LIKE THAT.
I TOLD HER SHE SHOULD GET SOME KIND OF PRIZE.
YOU TOLD HER...? YOU MEAN YOU'VE SEEN HER?
WHERE IS SHE? YOU'VE GOT TO TAKE ME THERE!
WELL, YEAH. I COULD DO THAT.
IT'S NOT FAR, WHEN YOU COME RIGHT DOWN TO IT.
YOU WANT TO COME THROUGH HERE. WE'LL BE THERE IN A NEW YORK MINUTE.

OH MY GOD! I LOOKED EVERYWHERE FOR MONA!
AND I COULD HAVE GONE AND ASKED YOU, ANY TIME!
WELL, NO.

NOT ANY TIME.

I'M REALLY SORRY, ELAINE. WHAT YOU GAVE HIM WAS LIFE, YOU KNOW?

THERE'S ONLY SO MUCH TO GO AROUND...
TO BE CONTINUED

AND THE HOUNDS CLOSED IN--
THEN YOU'RE POWERLESS WITHOUT THE FEATHERS?
LUCIFER, YOU'VE DESTROYED ME.
YOU'VE DESTROYED US ALL.
--WHICH MEANT THE HUNTERS WOULD BE ONLY MOMENTS BEHIND.
IT'S YOUR SCENT THEY FOLLOWED HERE. I COULD LEAVE YOU TO DIE.
YES. YOU COULD.
BUT THE CARDS WERE YOUR CREATION, MELEOS.
THAT'S REALLY WHY YOU'RE HERE, ISN'T IT? BECAUSE YOU FEEL RESPONSIBLE FOR ALL THIS.
KRITSCHH
AND POWERLESS IS A RELATIVE TERM.

I HAD NO PART IN YOUR MACHINATIONS. I STAYED ABOVE THE RUCK OF WAR.
I HARMED NO ONE!
OH LORD, THEY'RE COMING FOR US. WHAT MUST I DO NOW?
WHAT MUST I DO?
HOLD THEM OFF.
HOLD THEM OFF?
WHY, CERTES, MORNINGSTAR. FOR HOW LONG DO YOU WISH ME TO DELAY THEM?
"UNTIL YOU FALL," SAID LUCIFER.
PURGATORIO
MIKE CAREY WRITER PETER GROSS AND RYAN KELLY ARTISTS
COMICRAFT LETTERING DANIEL VOZZO COLORS AND SEPARATIONS
CHRISTOPHER MOELLER COVER PAINTER MARIAH HUEHNER ASSISTANT EDITOR
SHELLY BOND EDITOR • BASED ON CHARACTERS CREATED BY GAIMAN, KIETH AND DRINGENBERG
PART 3 OF 3

GOOD MORROW TO YOU, MAKER. WE HAD FORESEEN THAT WE WOULD MEET YOU AGAIN SOON.
THIS IS A FOOLISH CAUSE FOR AN ANGEL TO DIE IN.
YOU USED DOGS TO FIND US, BASANOS. SO OBVIOUSLY YOUR SIGHT IS DIM IN THIS PLACE.
PERHAPS IT'S NOT MY DEATH THAT LOOMS, BUT YOURS.
MAKER, WE ARE DEATH. WE CAN MAKE THE AIR CATCH FIRE AND THE MOUNTAINS SCREAM.
WE CAN SEEK OUT ALL YOUR POSSIBLE DOOMS AND BRING THEM DOWN UPON YOUR HEAD LIKE RAIN.
LAY ON, THEN.
I WILL NOT MOVE FROM THIS PLACE.
FOR YOU ARE MY SIN.
MINE ALONE.

NORTH LONDON.
OH JESUS. I DID THIS.
IT'S ALL MY FAULT.
I'M SORRY, MR. BELLOC, BUT FOR THE RECORD I NEED YOU TO SAY--
IT'S HER. IT'S OUR DAUGHTER, ELAINE.
I WAS SO COLD TO HER. THAT'S WHY SHE WAS STUDYING AT SARAH'S HOUSE.
TO--TO GET AWAY FROM ME.
WHAT HAPPENED, INSPECTOR DONOGHUE?
HOW DID SHE DIE?
WELL, SHE DIED WHEN THE ROOF FELL IN ON HER, MRS. BELLOC. CRUSH INJURY TO THE HEAD.
BUT THERE WERE WOUNDS ALL OVER HER BODY, AND THE BLOOD WORK CONFIRMS THAT SOME OF THAT WAS DONE AT THE FRIEND'S HOUSE.
THE OTHER TWO CHILDREN ARE CRITICALLY ILL, BUT THE ASSAILANT LEFT THEM WHERE THEY FELL.
HE CARRIED ELAINE INTO THE SUBWAY TUNNELS--PERHAPS THINKING HE WAS LESS LIKELY TO BE DISTURBED THERE.
OH. OH.
OH NO.
WHY DOES GOD LET THESE THINGS HAPPEN?

THE SILVER CITY.
FORGIVE US FOR INTRUDING ON YOUR INTROSPECTION, ARCHON--
--BUT THE NAME HAS SENT US TO SUMMON YOU.
INDEED?
THEN WHY ARE YOU AFRAID, SERAPHS, IF YOU ARE DOING AS GOD HAS BIDDEN YOU?
BECAUSE YOU ARE MICHAEL, AND WE WERE TOLD TO BRING YOU--
--WHETHER YOU WOULD OR NO.
AND IF I REFUSED?
HOW WOULD YOU CARRY OUT THESE ORDERS?
TRULY WE COULD NOT.
BUT GOD HAS COMMANDED, AND SO WE WOULD TRY. AND YOU WOULD DESTROY US.
WELL, IT WAS A FOOLISH QUESTION. LET US SEE WHAT SACRIFICE MY FATHER WOULD ASK OF ME THIS TIME.
AND WHAT GREAT PLANS HE HAS FOR US ALL.

THEY WERE RIGHT, OF COURSE.
I COULD NOT WIN.
IT WAS NOT THE WEIGHT OF NUMBERS THAT MATTERED.
IT WAS THE WEIGHT OF CHANCE.
THEIR HAND ON THE TILLER OF DESTINY, LEANING, LEANING.
UNTIL MY FALL BECAME NOT MERELY POSSIBLE, OR LIKELY, BUT INEVITABLE.
THE BLADE WAS AT MY THROAT. DEATH SNIGGERED--A FINAL VERDICT ON MY LIFE AND WORKS.
AND THEN--
--IMPOSSIBLY--
BROTHER, HOLD! HOLD AND LOOK UP.
THOSE ARE TRUMPETS.

--I WAS REDEEMED.

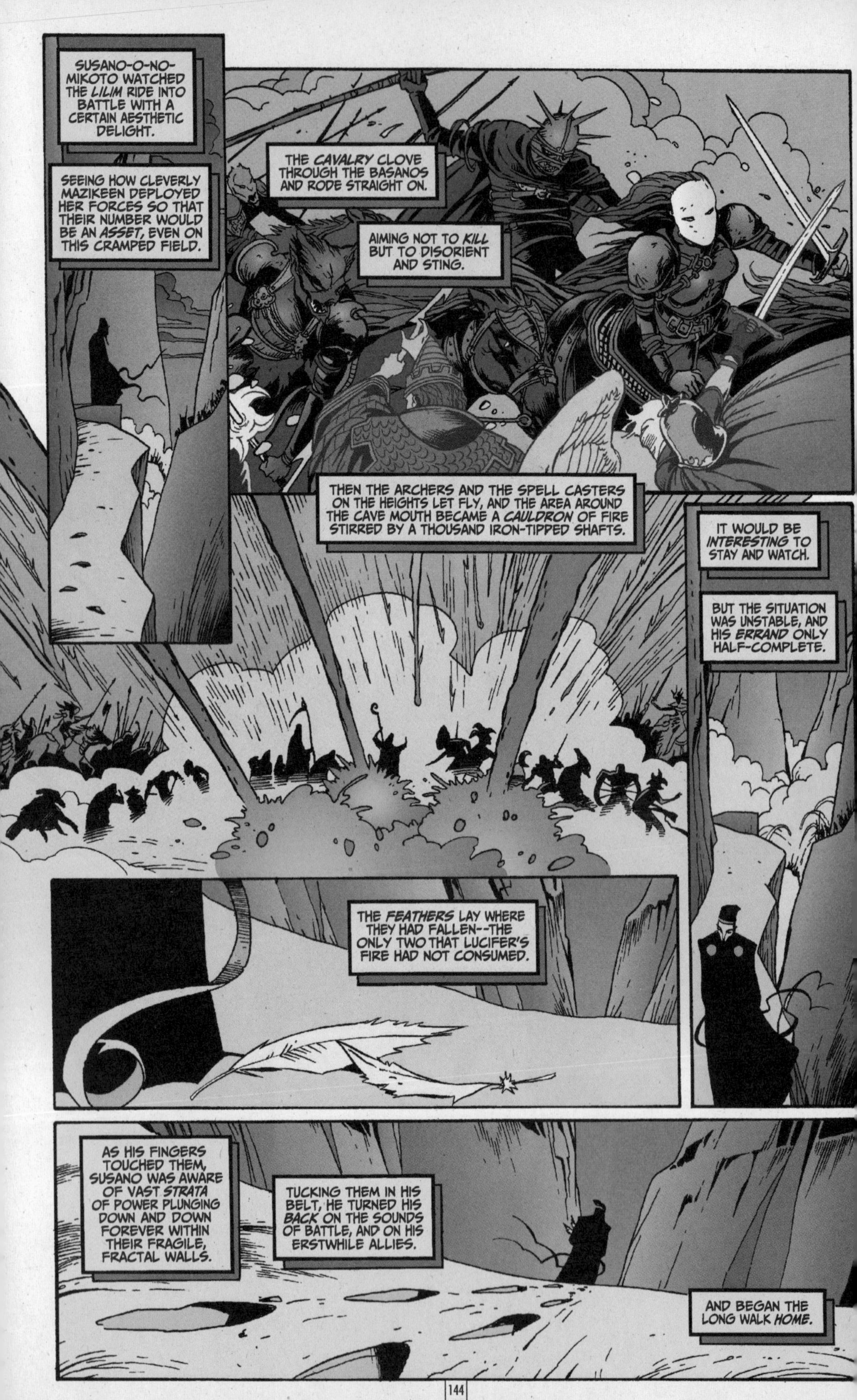
SUSANO-O-NO-MIKOTO WATCHED THE *LILIM* RIDE INTO BATTLE WITH A CERTAIN AESTHETIC DELIGHT.
SEEING HOW CLEVERLY MAZIKEEN DEPLOYED HER FORCES SO THAT THEIR NUMBER WOULD BE AN *ASSET*, EVEN ON THIS CRAMPED FIELD.
THE *CAVALRY* CLOVE THROUGH THE BASANOS AND RODE STRAIGHT ON.
AIMING NOT TO *KILL* BUT TO DISORIENT AND STING.
THEN THE ARCHERS AND THE SPELL CASTERS ON THE HEIGHTS LET FLY, AND THE AREA AROUND THE CAVE MOUTH BECAME A *CAULDRON* OF FIRE STIRRED BY A THOUSAND IRON-TIPPED SHAFTS.
IT WOULD BE *INTERESTING* TO STAY AND WATCH.
BUT THE SITUATION WAS UNSTABLE, AND HIS *ERRAND* ONLY HALF-COMPLETE.
THE *FEATHERS* LAY WHERE THEY HAD FALLEN--THE ONLY TWO THAT LUCIFER'S FIRE HAD NOT CONSUMED.
AS HIS FINGERS TOUCHED THEM, SUSANO WAS AWARE OF VAST *STRATA* OF POWER PLUNGING DOWN AND DOWN FOREVER WITHIN THEIR FRAGILE, FRACTAL WALLS.
TUCKING THEM IN HIS BELT, HE TURNED HIS *BACK* ON THE SOUNDS OF BATTLE, AND ON HIS ERSTWHILE ALLIES.
AND BEGAN THE LONG WALK *HOME*.

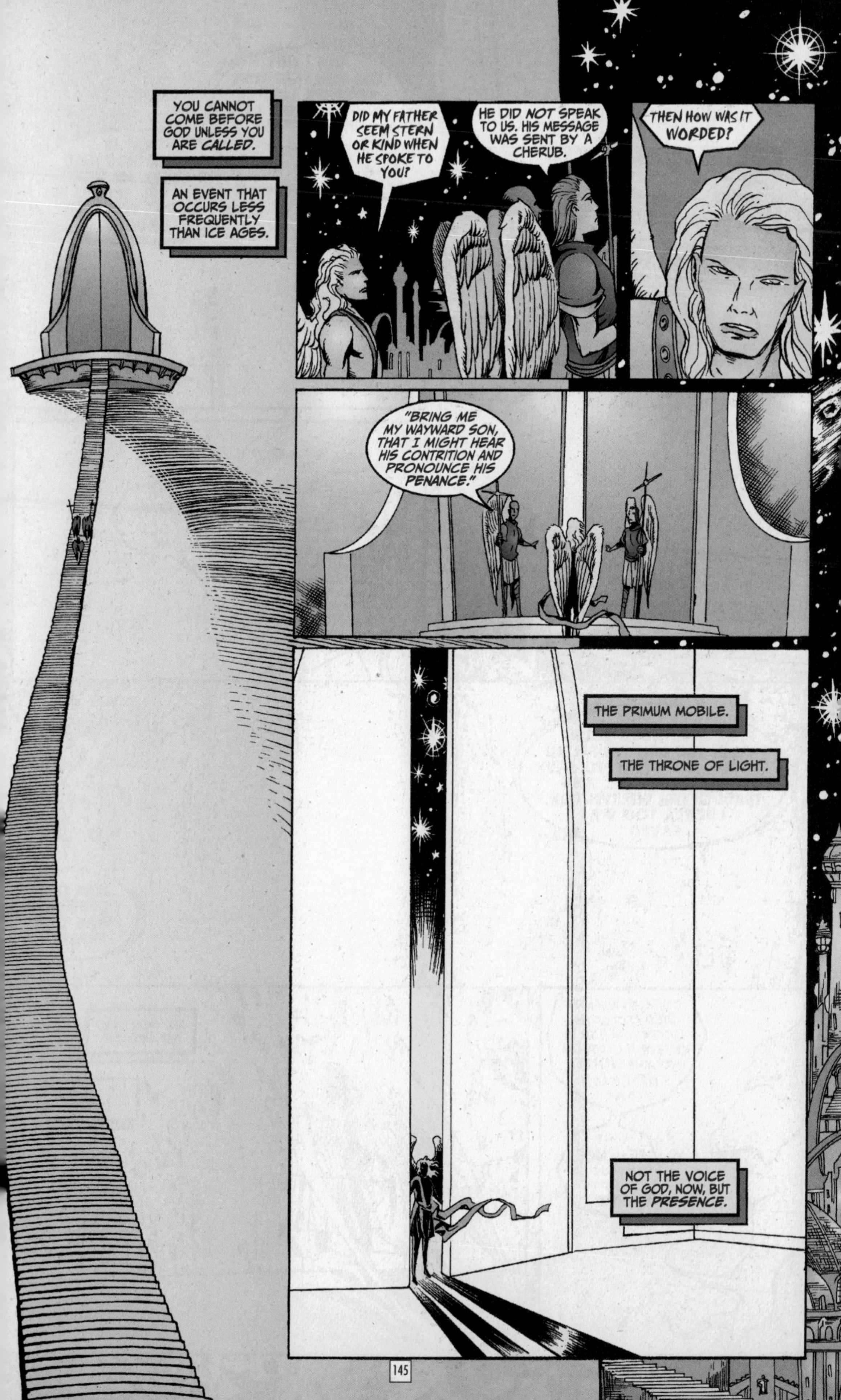
YOU CANNOT COME BEFORE GOD UNLESS YOU ARE *CALLED*.
AN EVENT THAT OCCURS LESS FREQUENTLY THAN ICE AGES.
DID MY FATHER SEEM STERN OR KIND WHEN HE SPOKE TO YOU?
HE DID *NOT* SPEAK TO US. HIS MESSAGE WAS SENT BY A CHERUB.
THEN HOW WAS IT *WORDED?*
"BRING ME MY WAYWARD SON, THAT I MIGHT HEAR HIS CONTRITION AND PRONOUNCE HIS PENANCE."
THE PRIMUM MOBILE.
THE THRONE OF LIGHT.
NOT THE VOICE OF GOD, NOW, BUT THE *PRESENCE*.

MICHAEL.
FATHER.
DID I NOT TELL YOU THAT YOUR BROTHER LUCIFER WAS GIVEN OVER TO DESTRUCTION?
THAT IF HEAVEN ONLY HELD ITS HAND, HE WOULD SURELY DIE, AND ALL HIS WORKS COME TO NAUGHT?
YES.
THAT IS WHAT YOU TOLD ME.
BUT YOU DID NOT HOLD YOUR HAND. YOU SENT THE FALLEN CHERUB GAUDIUM TO SAVE YOUR DAUGHTER. AND THROUGH HER INTERVENTION, LUCIFER TOO WAS SAVED.
WAS THIS OBEDIENCE? WAS THIS FEALTY?
FATHER, MY DAUGHTER DIED RESTORING LUCIFER TO HEALTH. IN SPITE OF ALL I DID, SHE DIED, AND EVEN HER SPIRIT IS LOST TO ME.
WHAT PENANCE CAN YOU FIND TO ADD TO THAT?
AND GOD GAVE HIS ANSWER.
AND MICHAEL WEPT.

IT WAS A BATTLE UNLIKE ANY I HAVE SEEN.
WITH AN ADVANTAGE OF A THOUSAND TO ONE-- BUT AGAINST A FOE WHO COULD NOT BE HURT.
WAR LEADER, THEY ARE RALLYING. OUR LOSSES ARE HEAVY.
I KNOW. TELL MISRAN TO HOLD THE LINE, ELOKIM SHAER. AND BRING DOWN THE PIKEMEN.
IN SUCH CIRCUMSTANCES, STRATEGY IS BORN OUT OF DESPERATION--AND ALL TOO SOON RETURNS THERE.
THEY'RE TRYING TO PIN US DOWN.
AND TO KEEP US FROM THE CAVE MOUTH. A REASONABLE STRATEGY, GIVEN THAT THEY CAN'T KILL US.
THE LILIM ARE BUYING TIME FOR THE MORNINGSTAR. USING THE ONLY COIN THEY HAVE.
UNDER THE CIRCUMSTANCES, A POOR BARGAIN.

KARAKOOOM
HALF THEIR *ARCHERS* IN ONE PASS. IMPRESSIVE.
A *SIDE EFFECT*, MERELY. AS I SAID, THEY'RE GUARDING THE CAVE MOUTH.
BUT THE BASANOS GOES WHERE IT *CHOOSES*.
COME, LUCIFER. TRADE *IRONIES* WITH US.
EXCORIATE US WITH YOUR RAPIER TONGUE.

THEY WERE BUYING HIM *DISTANCE*, NOT TIME.
HE'S GONE.

WAKE UP.

OH MY GOD! YOU!
AH, THEN YOU HEARD THE RUMORS OF MY DEATH.

LISTEN, IT... IT WASN'T ME. IT WAS THE CARDS. THEY JUST USED ME.
AND THEN THEY SCREWED ME, TOO. MADE ME PREGNANT. I CAN'T EVEN KILL MYSELF.

PERHAPS I CAN HELP YOU THERE.

THEIR LEAVING SUCKED ALL THE SOUND AND MOTION AFTER THEM.
THEY PASSED ON LIKE A STORM, TO SPEND THEIR FURY BEYOND THE HORIZON.
YOU FOUGHT ON LUCIFER'S SIDE, MAZIKEEN. I DID NOT EXPECT THAT.
NEITHER DID THE BASANOS. IT WAS A CALCULATED RISK.
BUT WHAT DO YOU GAIN IF HE SURVIVES?
EVERYTHING.
JUST ONE OF YOU.
THE REST CAN KEEP THEIR DISTANCE.

LUCIFER, THIS IS FARCICAL. YOU'RE STILL TOO WEAK TO FIGHT US.
AND THE VESSEL IS UNDER OUR AEGIS-- SAFE FROM ALL HARM.
SAFE, IS SHE? THEN YOU HAVE NOTHING TO WORRY ABOUT.
AND WHAT'S THE WORST THAT CAN HAPPEN? IN A HUNDRED MILLION YEARS OR SO, IF THE CONDITIONS ARE RIGHT, YOU CAN LAY ANOTHER EGG.
OH GOD! MAKE HIM STOP! KILL ME OR MAKE HIM STOP!
I CAN'T BEAR THIS MUCH PAIN!
WHAT IS YOUR OFFER?
ACTUALLY, IT'S MORE OF AN ULTIMATUM. EXTINGUISH YOURSELVES AND I'LL LET HER LIVE.
AND I'LL TAKE NO ACTION AGAINST YOUR OFFSPRING UNLESS IT THREATENS ME FIRST.

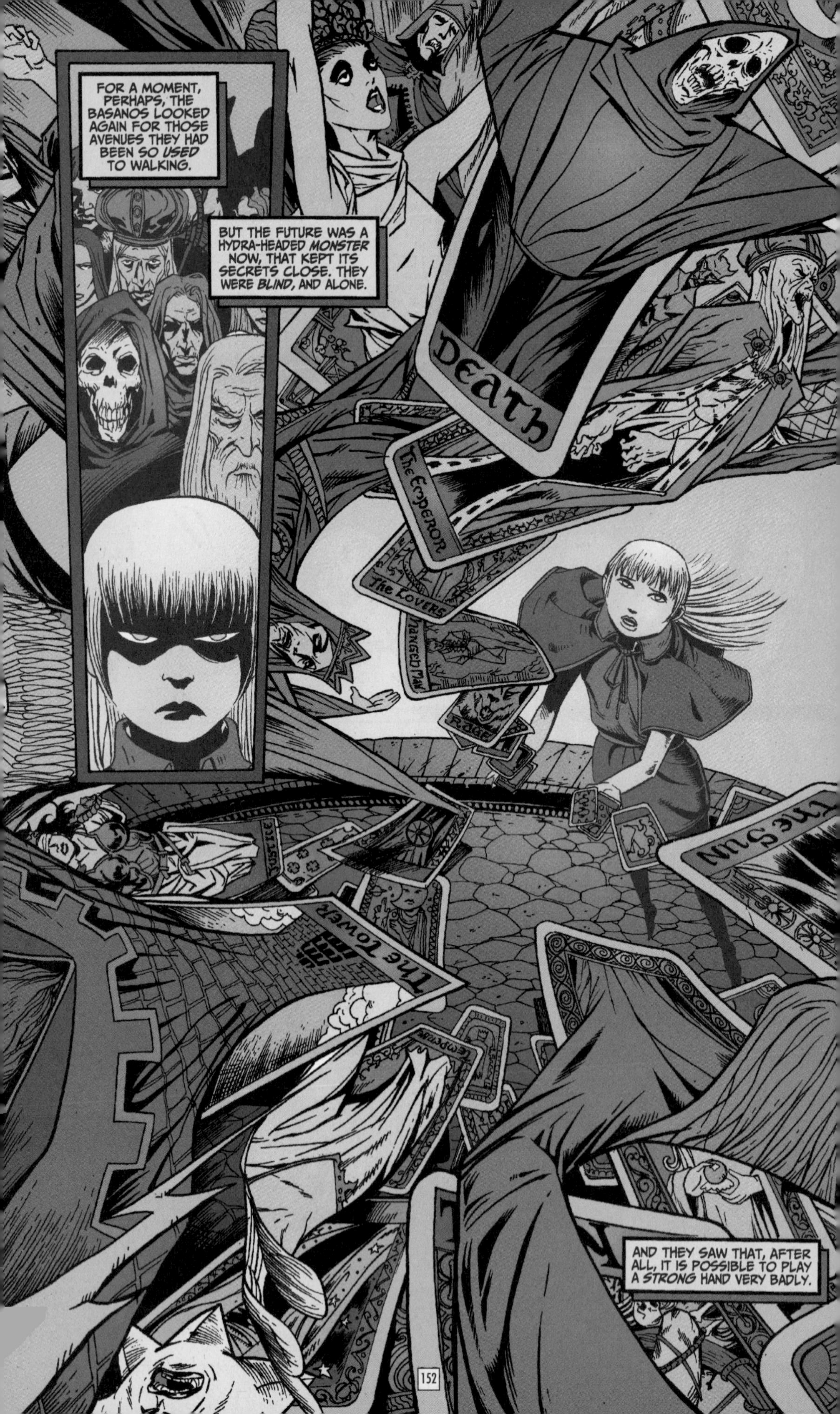
FOR A MOMENT, PERHAPS, THE BASANOS LOOKED AGAIN FOR THOSE AVENUES THEY HAD BEEN SO USED TO WALKING.
BUT THE FUTURE WAS A HYDRA-HEADED MONSTER NOW, THAT KEPT ITS SECRETS CLOSE. THEY WERE BLIND, AND ALONE.
DEATH
THE EMPEROR
THE LOVERS
HANGED MAN
RAGE
JUSTICE
THE SUN
THE TOWER
EMPRESS
AND THEY SAW THAT, AFTER ALL, IT IS POSSIBLE TO PLAY A STRONG HAND VERY BADLY.

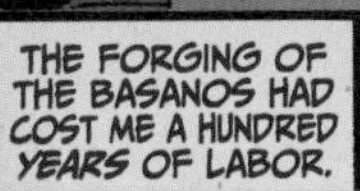
THE FORGING OF THE BASANOS HAD COST ME A HUNDRED YEARS OF LABOR.
I WOULD HAVE PREFERRED NOT TO BE PRESENT AT THEIR UNMAKING. BUT THE MORNINGSTAR'S INVITATION ALLOWED NO REFUSAL.

ALL THERE? ALL IN SUIT ORDER?
OR DO I NEED TO COUNT YOU?

NO. WE ARE ALL HERE.

YOUR UNIVERSE DOOMED US, LIGHTBRINGER. NOT YOUR WILL, OR YOUR INTELLECT.
IT DIMMED OUR SIGHT AND CONFUSED OUR STRATEGIES.

MY UNIVERSE EXPRESSES MY WILL.
DO YOU NEED A MATCH, BY ANY CHANCE?

AHHRRR!
STILL... WE MIGHT HAVE WON... IF YOUR STRENGTH HAD NOT RETURNED TO YOU.
WE SHOULD NOT HAVE BELIEVED... SUSANO'S ASSURANCES. WE ARE BEST... ALONE.
MY STRENGTH?
NO, THAT DIDN'T TURN OUT TO BE CRUCIAL, AFTER ALL.
BUT I COUNT MYSELF LUCKY THAT YOU'RE A TAROT DECK RATHER THAN A POKER DECK.
HEY, DON'T KNOCK MY PERFORMANCE.
I PUT MY HEART AND SOUL INTO THAT.
YOU THINK I'VE GOT A FUTURE ON THE LEGITIMATE STAGE?

THANK GOD. THANK GOD THAT'S OVER.
WE'LL TALK ABOUT IT LATER.
LUCIFER. MY ARM...YOU SAID--
FOR NOW, YOU'D BEST STAND AWAY FROM ME.
"IF I HAD INCURRED A DEBT, BELIEVE ME, I WOULD HAVE REMEMBERED."
YOUR WORDS.
I KNOW.
AND I AM... GRATEFUL FOR YOUR ASSISTANCE.
AS SOON AS I CAN, I WILL GIVE YOU BACK YOUR FACE.
AH.
YES.

I ASK THAT THE LILIM BE GRANTED A HOMELAND, HERE ON THIS WORLD. ACTING AS YOUR ARMY.
ENJOYING YOUR FAVOR AND YOUR PROTECTION.
YES, I GATHERED. AND I ADMIT DEFEAT.
YOU'VE GOT A REAL FLAIR FOR POLITICS, HAVEN'T YOU?
YOU HAVE ACCEPTED MY SWORD AND MY OATH, LORD. I AM YOUR SERVANT AGAIN. ALL MY SKILLS ARE YOURS TO COMMAND.
OH. HEY THERE.
LOOKIN' GOOD.
THUK
ONCE THE CHILD IS BORN, THE BLESSING OF THE BASANOS WILL PASS FROM YOU.
THAT IS WHEN I WILL FIND YOU. WHEN YOU CAN ONCE AGAIN BLEED AND DIE.

THE BRIEF BUT TERRIBLE REIGN OF THE BASANOS LEFT FEW MEMORIALS. THE LILIM DEALT WITH THE TOWER, AND THE RUINED CITIES WERE SIMPLY ABANDONED.

LUCIFER HAD OUTLAWED WORSHIP, BUT HE SAID NOTHING EITHER WAY ABOUT SUPERSTITION.

AS FOR THE MORNINGSTAR HIMSELF, HE HAD OTHER MATTERS TO SETTLE BEFORE HE LEFT.

HE SPOKE LONG AND LATE WITH THE MORTAL WOMAN, JILL PRESTO. I WAS NOT PRIVY TO THEIR COUNSELS.

THE GENERALS OF THE LILIM IN EXILE WERE ALSO SUMMONED TO HIM, AND DECAMPED SOON AFTER.
IT WAS ASSUMED THAT THEY HAD BEEN ENTRUSTED WITH AN ERRAND OF SOME DELICACY OR MOMENT.

ON THE MORNING OF HIS DEPARTURE, WE SPOKE ONE FINAL TIME--OF DEBT AND OBLIGATION, AND OF THE CHILD, ELAINE BELLOC.
HE HAD A MESSAGE FOR HER FATHER. SINCE I WAS INSTRUMENTAL IN HER DEATH HE BADE ME CARRY IT FOR HIM.

AND THEN HE LEFT THAT PLACE.

AND I CEASED TO BE HIS CHRONICLER.

SUSANO-O-NO-MIKOTO HAS LEFT LUCIFER'S COSMOS. HE IS NO LONGER SUBJECT TO ITS LAWS.
AND HE CARRIES AT HIS WAIST THE TWO FEATHERS WHICH HAVE BECOME THE REPOSITORIES OF THE MORNINGSTAR'S MIGHT AND MAJESTY.
IT FOLLOWS, THEN, THAT ANY ATTEMPT TO RETRIEVE THE FEATHERS MUST ALSO TAKE PLACE IN GOD'S CREATION.
IT IS THERE THAT THE LILIM HAVE GONE.
IT IS THERE, I AM SURE, THAT LUCIFER IS NOW TO BE FOUND.
FOR IT IS EXACTLY ONE YEAR, MEASURED BY THE TIME WE KNOW, SINCE THE MORNINGSTAR BEGAN HIS PERILOUS ENTERPRISE. AND EXACTLY A YEAR AGO, HE MADE A PROMISE.
SO POWERLESS AS HE NOW IS, HE NONETHELESS HAS AN APPOINTMENT TO KEEP--
--IN HELL.
THE END
next: BREAKING and ENTERING

"GOD? OH SHIT, YEAH. WE USED TO BE BIG, BIG FRIENDS OF HIS."
"REALLY?"
"YEAH, REALLY. BIG."
"THIS WAS WHEN THE FIRMAMENT ABOVE AND THE FIRMAMENT BELOW HADN'T BEEN DIVIDED YET.
"IN FACT, NOW THAT I THINK BACK, IT WAS ME WHO GAVE HIM THE IDEA FOR THAT.
"MY NAME WAS JOY.
"WITH MY SISTER HOPE AND MY BROTHER LIGHT, I CIRCLED THE DIVINE PRESENCE AND SANG ITS PRAISES.
"WE WERE ON FIRE. PERPETUALLY BURNING WITH THE LOVE OF THE NAME."
WELL THAT'S ALL VERY INTERESTING. NOT RELEVANT, PERHAPS, BUT INTERESTING.
PERPETUALLY BURNING YOU SAY?
THAT PROBABLY EXPLAINS WHY YOU LOOK LIKE THE KNOCKINGS THAT COME OUT OF MY PIPE.

LISTEN, PALLY? THIS HERE IS A FUCKING MARKET, RIGHT?
WE CAN TAKE OUR TRADE WHEREVER WE LIKE. SO LESS OF THE SMART MOUTH.

YOU'RE FALLEN CHERUBS. YOU HAVE THE TAINT OF HELL.
MOST FAIRIES WILL SHUN YOU.
OH YEAH? WELL THAT'S WHERE YOU'RE--

HEY, SPERA, ARE YOU NUTS OR SOMETHING?
KEEP YOUR THIEVING PAWS TO YOURSELF!
OW!

WHAT'D YOU HIT ME FOR, GAUDIUM?
YOUR OWN GOOD. THEY GOT LAWS HERE.
YOU STEAL SO MUCH AS A PIN FROM THIS GUY, HE CAN MAKE YOU WIPE HIS ASS WITH YOUR TONGUE FOR THE NEXT FIFTY YEARS.

MAYBE YOU SHOULD TELL HIM THAT YOU DO THAT STUFF FOR FREE.
IN FRONT OF A STRANGER YOU'RE SAYING THIS TO ME?
AHEM.

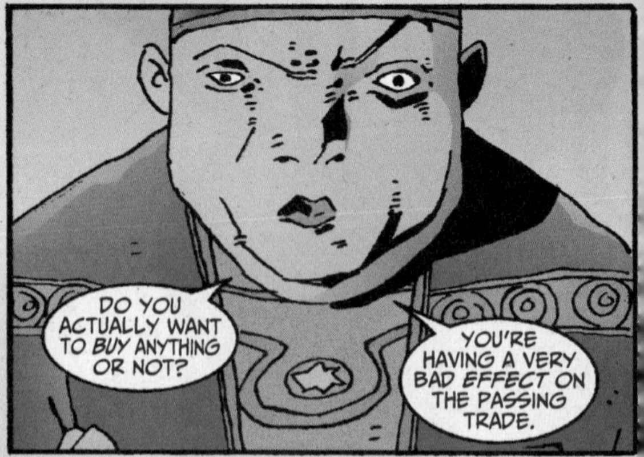
DO YOU ACTUALLY WANT TO BUY ANYTHING OR NOT?
YOU'RE HAVING A VERY BAD EFFECT ON THE PASSING TRADE.

OH, GOD-FOR-FUCKING-BID. OKAY THEN, PRETTY BOY, GIVE US A ROPE A THOUSAND MILES LONG. BETTER MAKE THAT GOSSAMER--
--A PREGNANT AKBITUR--
--AND THE OIL OF THE AMARANTHINE XAR.
TO GO.
HEY, ARE YOU SURE THAT AKBITUR IS PREGNANT?
WELL, SHE'S KNITTING LITTLE WOOLEN BOOTIES.
AND LAST NIGHT SHE WAS LOOKING AT A BOOK OF BABY NAMES.
BREAKING & ENTERING
MIKE CAREY WRITER DEAN ORMSTON ARTIST
COMICRAFT LETTERING DANIEL VOZZO COLORS AND SEPARATIONS
CHRISTOPHER MOELLER COVER PAINTER
MARIAH HUEHNER ASSISTANT EDITOR SHELLY BOND EDITOR
BASED ON CHARACTERS CREATED BY GAIMAN, KIETH & DRINGENBERG
"YOU GOT THE TAINT OF HE-ELL!"
DAMN SMARTASS FAIRY. THINKS HE OWNS THE FUCKING PLACE.
WELL, TECHNICALLY...

THE REALMS OF PAIN. SOME TIME LATER.
LUMEN? NAH, I THINK HE TOLD MOM THAT YOU AND ME DIED OR SOMETHING. HE'S SO FUCKING HOLIER THAN THOU.
WELL HE IS HOLIER. HE NEVER FELL.

HEY, SPERA. YOU'RE SURE OF YOUR FACTS, RIGHT?
OH, JESUS, AGAIN WITH THIS.
TRUST YOUR BIG SISTER, GAUDIUM. SHE WORKS FOR HER CUT.

"IN THE HOUSE OF THE SLEEPER, UNDER THE DREAD ABYSS, LIES THE BODY OF ERITI. SPEAK YOUR WISH INTO HER EAR AND IT WILL BE GRANTED."
"BE IT TO MAKE SURE THE SUN RUN BACKWARDS IN ITS COURSE, OR THE DEAD TO LIVE AGAIN." UNQUOTE.

OOH! OOH! YOU HEAR THAT? A BIRD SINGING OUT AMIDST THE DESOLATION.
IT'S A MIRACLE.

THE MIRACLE CALLED SUPPER.

SO YOU STILL REMEMBER THOSE "PRAISE THE LORD" DAYS, HUH?
SURE I REMEMBER. WHAT, YOU DON'T?
YOU GOT ALZHEIMER'S ALL OF A SUDDEN?

NO. BUT IT WAS A CROCK OF SHIT, IS ALL.
THE LOVE OF THE NAME. TCH, YEAH! SING EVERY HYMN YOU KNOW THEN START AGAIN FROM THE TOP.

SO WHEN LUCIFER MADE HIS PITCH, I WAS OF A MIND TO LISTEN.
OH YEAH!

"IF I'D HAD EYES BACK THEN, I WOULD HAVE BEEN STARING MOODILY INTO HIS.
"STEAD OF BOBBING UP AND DOWN LIKE A CHEAP SPECIAL EFFECT."

LOOK, CHERUBS ARE SPHERICAL BECAUSE IT'S A PERFECT PLATONIC SHAPE.
YOU KNOW THAT, RIGHT?
WHAT?

MMMMMMMMMMMMMM
BUT THERE ARE SO MANY TANGENTS. SO MANY CHOICES.
SO MANY POSSIBILITIES THAT OPEN UP ONCE THE STERILITY OF PERFECTION IS RENOUNCED.

WELL ANY WAY YOU LOOK AT IT, LUCIFER *STIFFED* US.
HE DID *NOT!*
OH, STOP THINKING WITH YOUR *SEX* AND SMELL THE SCORCHED BIRD!

HE SAID WE SHOULD CHOOSE OUR OWN *DESTINY,* RIGHT?
SO HOW DID THAT LEAD TO US STORMING HEAVEN WITH "I LOVE LUCIFER" *T-SHIRTS* ON?

"THERE WERE FRIGGING ARCHANGELS TEARING *PIECES* OUT OF EACH OTHER. SERAPHS IN BATTLE WAGONS PULLED BY SEVEN-HEADED ALLEGORICAL *BEASTS.*

"CONGRATULATIONS! WE'VE DECIDED TO GIVE YOU LIBERTY *AND* DEATH."

UH... YOU WANNA TOSS A *COIN* FOR FIRST WATCH?
NO!

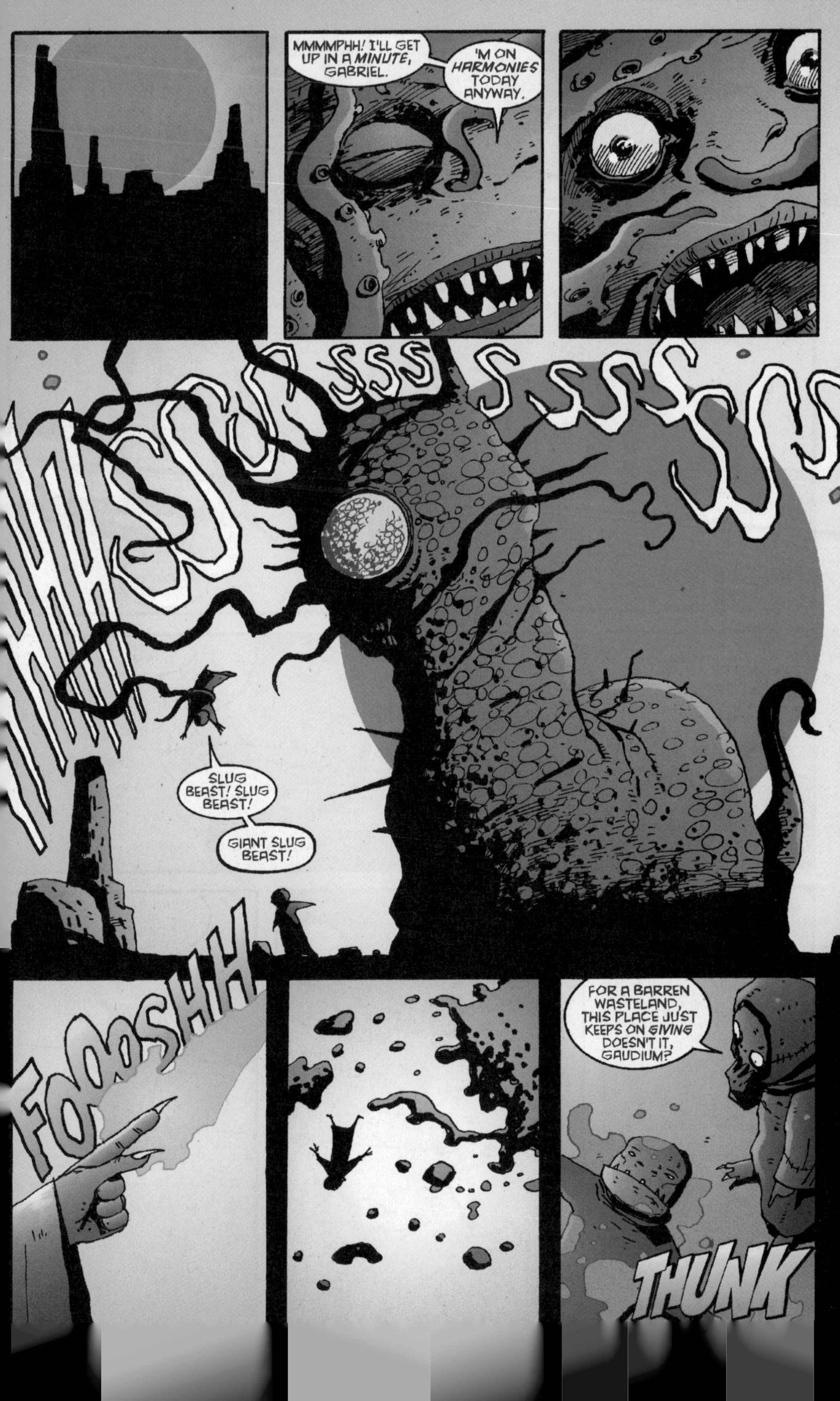
MMMMPHH! I'LL GET UP IN A *MINUTE*, GABRIEL.
'M ON *HARMONIES* TODAY ANYWAY.
HHHSSSSSSSSSSSSSS
SLUG BEAST! SLUG BEAST!
GIANT SLUG BEAST!
FOOOSHH
FOR A BARREN WASTELAND, THIS PLACE JUST KEEPS ON *GIVING* DOESN'T IT, GAUDIUM?
THUNK

WHY DO YOU NEED A RESURRECTION MAGIC, ANYWAY?
CAN'T YOU JUST BRING THIS LITTLE BRAT BACK AS A ZOMBIE OR A GHOST?
IT'S KINDA HARD TO EXPLAIN.

SHE IS MY CHILD, GAUDIUM. MY ONLY DAUGHTER.
PROTECT ELAINE AND I WILL PLEAD FOR YOU BEFORE MY FATHER'S THRONE.
A FULL PARDON, RIGHT?

OH, OKAY. PLEA BARGAINING. I GET IT NOW.
YEAH. NO. I DUNNO.

SHE'S AN AMAZING KID, AND WE WENT THROUGH SOME WEIRD SHIT TOGETHER.
AND I THINK IT STINKS THE WAY MELEOS USED HER. I SORT OF FEEL--

I DON'T BELIEVE IT! THAT'S A BLUSH!
MY BROTHER IS BLUSHING!

GAUDIUM'S GOT A GI-IRLFRIEND! GAUDIUM'S GOT A GI-IRLFRIEND!
OH FUCK YOU, SPERA!

IN DUE COURSE--
OKAY, THAT'S IT.
THE DREAD ABYSS.

WOW. PRETTY DREAD. TELL ME AGAIN WHY WE CAN'T JUST FLY DOWN?
BECAUSE THE BEATING OF OUR WINGS WOULD WAKE THE SLEEPER. AND ALL KNOWN SOURCES SAY THAT'S A TERMINALLY BAD IDEA.
COME ON, IT'S ONLY A THOUSAND MILES DOWN.

FAIRY GOSSAMER. EWWWWW!
HOW CAN YOU TRUST A SPECIES THAT WOULD MILK A SPIDER'S ASS?
YOU'VE DONE WORSE THINGS TO A SPIDER'S ASS.

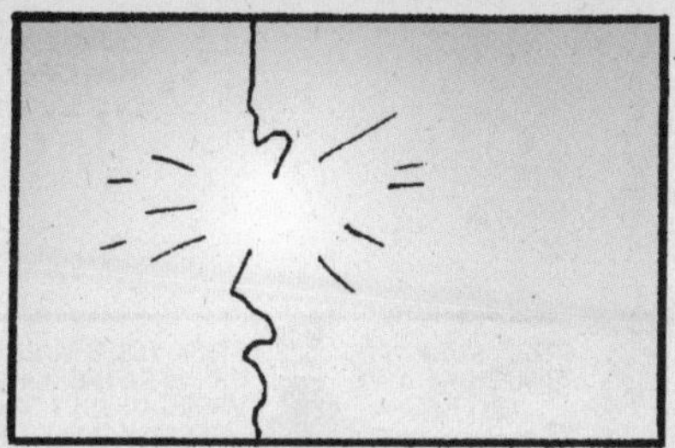

SHIT.

"THE BEST THERE IS."
"UNBREAKABLE."
WELL OBVIOUSLY YOU PISSED HIM OFF.

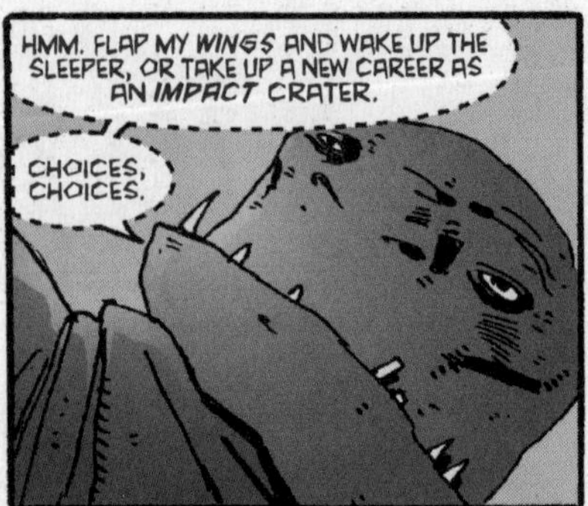
HMM. FLAP MY WINGS AND WAKE UP THE SLEEPER, OR TAKE UP A NEW CAREER AS AN IMPACT CRATER.
CHOICES, CHOICES.

STOP SULKING, GAUDIUM. I'VE GOT IT.
STICK YOUR WINGS OUT CROSSWISE, LIKE THE VANES OF A SYCAMORE SEED. YOU'LL SPIN DOWN.

THIS IS ACTUALLY FUN!
IT'S FUCKING HUMILIATING, IS WHAT IT IS.

THE SPINNING GOT TO YOU, HUH?
WELL, WHEN YOU'RE FINISHED PRAYING TO THE GREAT GOD HWLLCHH, TAKE A LOOK OVER THERE.
HWLLLLLLCHHHH!

THE HOUSE OF THE SLEEPER. YOU WERE RIGHT!
LIKE ALWAYS. LOOKS KIND OF FAUX *VICTORIAN*, DOESN'T IT?
LIKE SOMETHING OUT OF LORD DUNSANY.

AND THIS THING WILL REALLY EAT OUT THE LOCKS?

IF IT'S FEMALE AND PREGNANT IT WILL. THAT'S WHERE THEY NEST.
IF IT'S MALE, OF COURSE, IT'LL--

CHOMP

NNNNNGGGGGNNNNN!
WELL ACTUALLY IT WILL EAT YOUR WHOLE ARM OFF.
THEY HAVE AN INCREDIBLE APPETITE.

AND THEN IT'LL SING TO ATTRACT A MATE.
THAT'S WHEN WE COULD BE IN TROUBLE.
GUUUUUH!

WHUK WHUK! WH

WHUK! WHU
I'LL GO LOOK FOR ANOTHER WAY IN.
TRY TO KEEP THE NOISE DOWN.

WELL, WHAT DO YOU THINK?
WHAT DO I THINK?
I THINK IT'S A CAT FLAP, SPERA. A CAT FLAP TEN FEET HIGH.
OKAY. THAT'S WHAT I THOUGHT TOO.
BUT THE SLEEPER'S PET IS BLIND. IT HUNTS BY SMELL.
THE OIL OF AMARANTHINE XAR WILL DISGUISE YOUR SCENT.
OIL. OIL. OIL. OH, OKAY.
REMEMBER, I GET ANYTHING ELSE YOU FIND.
I'LL STAY OUTSIDE AND KEEP WATCH IN CASE--
OH, EFFRUL'S BALLS! WHAT'S THAT SMELL?
DOG TURDS. RENDERED BASILISK FAT. MAYBE SOME DEMON PUKE.
IF I GET OUT OF THIS ALIVE, I'M GOING BACK TO THAT MARKET WITH A RAILROAD SPIKE.

NOW YOU'RE GONNA SEE LOTS OF AMAZING THINGS IN HERE, BROTHER MINE.
LUCKY ME.
BUT TRY TO STAY ON COURSE. YOU'RE LOOKING FOR THE SLEEPER'S BED-CHAMBER.

"THERE'S A ROOM WHERE THE CANDLES BURN BACKWARDS. GET THROUGH THAT AS QUICKLY AS YOU CAN.
"AND WHATEVER YOU DO, DON'T BLOW ANY OF THEM OUT.

"IGNORE THE FRUIT OF ENTRANCING FRAGRANCE.

"IT'S THERE FOR A PURPOSE.

"ONLY TREAD ON THE STAIRS THAT ALREADY HAVE BODIES LYING ON THEM.
"THEIR POISON SACS ARE MORE LIKELY TO BE EMPTY.

"TAKE THE FIRST LEFT AFTER THE BATHROOM, THE LEGENDS SAY (IF YOU HEAR A NOISE LIKE A FAUCET DRIPPING, DON'T LOOK)--
"--AND YOU WILL COME TO THE CHAMBER OF THE SLEEPER."

FOUR-POSTER BED.
HOW FUCKING OSTENTATIOUS CAN YOU GET?

KREAK!

YES!
WE'VE HIT THE MOTHER LODE!

SSSSSSsss
HOLY MOTHER OF FUCK!
WHAT'S THAT? WHO'S THERE?
IS IT THE END OF THE WORLD ALREADY?

SHOOOM
FLAP
I'VE GOT SOME GOOD NEWS AND SOME BAD NEWS.
THE GODDESS ERITI! YOU DID IT!
FLAP
FLAP
FLAP
YEP. NOW LOOK DOWN.
FLAP
FLAP!
FLAP!
SKREEEEEEEEE
SKR

WHAT DID YOU DO?
I JUST SWORE LOUDLY.
DON'T GO ON ABOUT IT, OKAY? I'VE GOT IT COVERED.

ALL RIGHT, YOU PISS-SMELLING PIECE OF RUG!
YOU'RE ABOUT TO HAVE A HAIRBALL MOMENT.

GLLLK

COME ON, BROTHER.
PUNCH 'IM IN THE ESOPHAGUS! TIE HIS TONSILS IN A BOW!
HAK!
HAK!
RIP HIS--

--UH...

OH MY.

SKREEEEEEEEE
KKKT!
OH GOD, YOU SAVED MY LIFE!
WHAT CAN I EVER DO TO REPAY YOU, MICHAEL?

THREE TEAS. TWO BACON BUTTIES.

COSTELLA CAFE

SO THEN I THOUGHT, "MICHAEL WILL BE RELYING ON *ME* TO CLEAR THIS MESS UP."

"SO I'LL JUST GO PICK UP THE MUMMIFIED *CORPSE* OF THE GODDESS ERITI..."

YES. I UNDERSTAND.

IT WILL **NOT WORK,** I'M AFRAID, BUT IT WAS A VALIANT EFFORT.

AN ANGEL'S SPIRIT IS NOT **LIKE** THAT OF A MORTAL CHILD.

AND ERITI'S REACH IS NOT NEARLY LONG ENOUGH.

IT'S NOT? GREAT *RESEARCH,* SPERA.
HEY, YOU NEVER *SAID* THIS KID WAS AN ANGEL.
I NEVER SAID SHE *WASN'T.*

UH... SO... THAT ASIDE--
HOW ARE THINGS WITH YOU? YOU KNOW. GENERALLY?

MY FATHER HAS CAST ME FORTH FROM HEAVEN, AND FROM THE PERFECTION OF HIS LOVE.
I AM **EXILED.**

OH.
YOU KNOW, TODAY HAS SUCKED IN SO MANY WAYS.

BUT COME. WE ARE THE AUTHORS OF OUR OWN LIVES, AND DESPAIR IS THE ONLY UNPARDONABLE SIN.
THE DANCE GOES ON.
YEAH. YEAH, I GUESS.

I THANK YOU, LADY, FOR THE WARMTH AND COMFORT YOU HAVE OFFERED US.
UH... YOU'RE WELCOME.
THIS IS MY NUMBER, CUTIE. YOU DON'T DIAL IT, YOU JUST INTONE IT.

HEY. GAUDIUM--YOU OVERTIPPED!
I DIDN'T HAVE ANYTHING SMALLER.
...
The End

The Divine Cover Gallery
Art by Christopher Moeller

THE LUCIFER LIBRARY

OTHER TITLES FROM THE WORLD OF THE SANDMAN:

THE SANDMAN LIBRARY

THE SANDMAN: PRELUDES & NOCTURNES
Neil Gaiman/Sam Kieth/Mike Dringenberg/Malcolm Jones, III

THE SANDMAN: THE DOLL'S HOUSE
Neil Gaiman/Mike Dringenberg/Various

THE SANDMAN: DREAM COUNTRY
Neil Gaiman/Various

THE SANDMAN: SEASON OF MISTS
Neil Gaiman/Kelley Jones/Various

THE SANDMAN: A GAME OF YOU
Neil Gaiman/Shawn McManus/Various

THE SANDMAN: BRIEF LIVES
Neil Gaiman/Jill Thompson/Vince Locke

THE SANDMAN: FABLES AND REFLECTIONS
Neil Gaiman/Various

THE SANDMAN: WORLDS' END
Neil Gaiman/Various

THE SANDMAN: THE KINDLY ONES

THE SANDMAN: THE WAKE
Neil Gaiman/Michael Zulli/Jon J Muth/Charles Vess

DEATH: THE HIGH COST OF LIVING
Neil Gaiman/Chris Bachalo/Mark Buckingham

DEATH: THE TIME OF YOUR LIFE
Neil Gaiman/Chris Bachalo/Mark Buckingham

DESTINY: A CHRONICLE OF DEATHS FORETOLD
Alisa Kwitney/Various

THE SANDMAN: THE DREAM HUNTERS
Neil Gaiman/Yoshitaka Amano

THE SANDMAN: DUST COVERS — THE COLLECTED SANDMAN COVERS
Neil Gaiman/Dave McKean

THE SANDMAN COMPANION
Hy Bender

THE QUOTABLE SANDMAN
Neil Gaiman/Various

THE SANDMAN PRESENTS: THE FURIES
Mike Carey/John Bolton